Home for Good

HOMEMAKING SIMPLICITY

AND

CONTENTMENT

Linda C. Shields

ISBN-13: 978-1515359623

ISBN-10: 151535962X

LCCN: 2015916571

BISAC: HOM019000
House & Home / Cleaning, Caretaking & Organizing

Linda C. Shields, Eureka, Missouri, USA

WWW.LINDASHIELDS.COM

DEDICATION

To Steven, who makes it possible for me to be a homemaker and a happy wife, and to all of our children and grandchildren, who give us such joy. Everything I do is all about you.

ACKNOWLEDGEMENTS

Without the selfless editorial and publishing assistance of my dear friend Christi Checkett, this book would still be unfinished.

Without the encouragement and devotion of my husband it would never have begun.

I thank the Lord for you both.

CONTENTS

INTRODUCTION 1

CHAPTER 1

WHAT IS A HOMEMAKER?...7

  The Homemaker Defined 10

CHAPTER 2

NEVER CLEAN FOR COMPANY...17

  How to Clean Like a Pro...19

    Dust...24

    Clean the Floors...25

    Clean the Kitchen..26

    Clean the Bathroom 26

    Daily Maintenance Walk-Through 28

      Action Assignments 31

CHAPTER 3

NO MORE SPRING CLEANING 33

  Suggestions for Every Room...36

    Suggestions for the Bathroom...39

    Suggested Bathroom Rules...41

    Suggestions for the Master Bedroom.....................................41

    Suggestions for the Children's Bedrooms..............................42

    Special Projects for Family Rooms..43

    Special Projects for the Dining Room 43

    Special Projects for the Kitchen..44

    Special Projects for the Basement...45

Special Projects for the Garage 46

    Action Assignments 48

CHAPTER 4

GETTING IT TOGETHER **49**

Your Receipt Box..50

Your Toolbox 51

Your Errand Bag..52

Your Decorating Kit 53

Your Check-Out Book..54

Your First Aid Center 54

Your Cleaning Center 56

Your Family Message Center 57

The Babysitter Book..58

Keys, Please!...59

    Action Assignments 61

CHAPTER 5

YOUR CONTROL CENTER...**63**

Finding a Place..63

Furnishing Your Office 65

Your Filing System 67

Gifty Bags 71

    Action Assignments 73

CHAPTER 6

CLASSY CLOSETS **75**

Make the Investment 76

Getting Started...79

Try On Everything...80

Contents

Your Want List 83

Stretch Your Budget 85

    Action Assignments 88

CHAPTER 7

ARE OUR HOURS OURS?...**89**

Your Datebook 90

Cultivating a Quiet Time 92

Managing Your Minutes...95

    Action Assignments 97

CHAPTER 8

GRACIOUS GIFT GIVING **99**

Make a Gift Budget 101

Make a Gift Notebook...102

Shop in Advance 103

Give Creative Gifts 104

Make a Gift Center 106

    Action Assignments 108

CHAPTER 9

CURB APPEAL **109**

    Action Assignments 116

CHAPTER 10

ORGANIZED CHILDREN? **117**

Abdicating Responsibility? 117

How to Teach Your Children...118

What About Discipline?...121

Sow Good Seed 122

Action Assignments 126

CHAPTER 11

HOW TO HANDLE A HUSBAND...**127**

Following God's Order...127

What Every Husband Craves 129

An Ungodly Woman's Influence 131

God's Mandate for Husbands.................................132

Motivating Your Spouse...132

Put it in Perspective..135

Action Assignments 137

CHAPTER 12

FEEDING YOUR FAMILY...**139**

Organization in the Kitchen.................................140

Menu Planning 143

Grocery Shopping 144

Meal Preparation..148

Action Assignments 151

CHAPTER 13

TIME FOR YOU..**153**

Level One: Physical Needs 153

We Are What We Eat...154

Burning Calories at Home 155

It's Okay to Nap..156

Who's In Control?...157

Level Two: Mental/Emotional Needs 159

Level Three: Spiritual Needs................................161

INTRODUCTION

"Lord, what on earth is the matter with me?" I muttered. I was having one of those discussions with God that I often have in frustrating moments. As I weaved my way through the bustling morning traffic on my way to work, nothing seemed at all right. I was growing more and more dissatisfied with life in the fast track. With a house, a husband, two teenage sons and one dog besides my full-time job, I was always rushing.

"Here I am complaining when you've given me the job I always thought I wanted. I have a management position, my own office, and I work with nice people—and yet I'm not satisfied. Why am I really happy only when I'm home?"

Suddenly God did something that never ceases to surprise me—He answered my question! Not audibly, but in that *"still, small voice"* that emanates from within, I heard a statement that I knew didn't come from myself.

"Listen to your heart!"

The thought startled me. Listen to my heart? What did that mean? Then I remembered one of my favorite scripture verses, *"Delight yourself in the Lord; and He will give you the desires of your heart"* (Psalm 37:4). Could it be that I had just admitted that being at home full-time was my heart's desire?

I had spent the earliest years of my marriage at home, feeling that our children needed a mother during their formative years more than we needed extra income. When they started attending school I began working outside the home, mostly on a part-time basis. But now I was working more and enjoying it less. I no longer had the time or the energy to do the things at home that I felt were important, and it left me feeling very unfulfilled. Or dissatisfied. Or like something wasn't quite right.

Then that inner voice spoke again.

1

"Why do you think you are happiest when you are in your own home? Why do you think that you are most content when you're working there? Don't you realize that that contentment comes from Me? I put that desire in you Myself! Don't think it's something wrong with you—it's something right with you to be most satisfied when you are working in your own home."

Suddenly I realized that my deep-seated love of taking care of my family and my home was, indeed, a desire that God Himself had deposited in my heart. Thinking about that made all the pieces fit together— the great sense of security and contentment that I always drew from working in my home came from being where God had created me to fit the best. When I was happy and secure, I was able to create a serene, tranquil atmosphere inside my home. That, in turn, made our home a welcome refuge for my husband and children when they returned there from a busy, tiring, or stressful day. It all made perfect sense. I understood. A home is not a home without a homemaker! It is a house. Or a hotel. *But only a real homemaker can make it a home.*

When I, too, came home after an exhausting day at work, no one else was there to minister peace and healing to any of us. That's why God was sweetly encouraging me to make our home a haven for us, so I could function as the *"foot washer,"* much like Jesus washed the feet of His disciples, cleansing them of the dust they had picked up while walking through a dirty world.

I also began to see the wisdom of Paul's words, telling women to be *"workers at home,"* or as the King James Version puts it, *"keepers at home."* (Titus 2:5) Perhaps this command was just as inspired as the rest of the Bible, and not just some cultural standard of Paul's day? Perhaps it was written not only for the benefit of the family, but also for the benefit of the woman herself? Perhaps working at home fulfills that desire that is built into our very genetic makeup. Those double X chromosomes every woman carries aren't there just to make us love shopping and wearing pretty things--they make us *"X-cellent"* home managers!

As I pondered those things in my heart over the next few weeks, at work I also began an informal survey of my female co-workers. I started asking them during conversations, *"If money was not a factor and you could do anything you wanted to do, would you continue in your job or would you prefer to stay home?"*

I was surprised by their candidness. The overwhelming majority responded with an immediate, *"I would stay home in a minute!"* Most of them also said, *"I like my job, and I derive some satisfaction from it. But I would love more than anything to stay home."* Rare was the woman who said, *"Oh, I'd be too bored. I would rather go to work every day than stay home."* But there were a few for whom boredom was a real fear. I knew from personal experience that boredom was never a problem for me—I could always think of endless ways to keep myself occupied at home, even more than at a *"real"* job!

One woman, who had to enter the work force after a divorce, impressed me with how deeply the home itself ministers peace and security to a woman's heart. She said, *"When I first started working, I missed my home so much that every day I spent my thirty minute lunch break just going home. It took me ten minutes to drive there, and ten minutes to drive back to work, which only gave me ten minutes to be home. That didn't even allow me time to eat, but I didn't care. It just felt so good to sit there for ten minutes! It helped me get through the rest of the day. If I still worked that close to home, I would still be doing it today. After all these years of having to support myself, I miss being a homemaker more than anything."*

Economics seemed to be the major obstacle to staying home for most women. So many women were divorced, most with children to support, and they had no choice about working outside the home unless they wanted to simply be poor welfare recipients. Few such women were fortunate enough to have home-based paying careers, but in today's technological world a home-based business is more and more feasible. Often these working women were married, but thought that their husband's income was inadequate to support their family. I wondered how many of those had actually ever

3

sat down and really calculated what it cost them to go to work away from home every day. After the expense of child care, clothing, transportation, meals eaten out, and extra spending because *"after all, we have two incomes,"* sometimes a wife and mother's outside income is actually a net loss. And there were also women, like myself, who felt a little guilty about staying home and worked simply to augment the family income and provide for those little luxuries that we all enjoy. It might be a small sacrifice to do without the extras that a job provided, but it could be done without a major hardship.

In fact, as women return to their homes, they often find that they are actually financially better off. According to author Marcus Buckingham,* *"All told, more than 1.3 million men and women have been surveyed over the last 40 years, both here in the U.S. and in developed countries around the world. Wherever researchers have been able to collect reliable data on happiness, the finding is always the same: greater educational, political, and employment opportunities have corresponded to decreases in life happiness for women, as compared to men. Since 1972, women's overall level of happiness has dropped, both relative to where they were forty years ago, and relative to men. You find this drop in happiness in women regardless of whether they have kids, how many kids they have, how much money they make, how healthy they are, what job they hold, whether they are married, single or divorced, how old they are, or what race they are."*

Although secular researchers have finally admitted that women are increasingly unhappy with the world's system of finding *"success"*, they are still apparently puzzled as to why. Yet they cannot deny that the *"feminist"* dream of the 1960's has now been tried for decades, and found wanting. In the long run, the more women focus upon life satisfaction outside their home, the less happy they admit that they are. Realizing these things helped me realize that I wanted to change direction and priorities.

When I approached my husband with the idea of my staying home full-time, I was surprised by his response. *"That's fine with me. By the time you subtract taxes and expenses from your paycheck, it's hardly worth all the inconvenience it causes the whole family."* That was all the encouragement I needed to go where my heart lead me.

This book is written for every woman who has been blessed with the freedom to leave the world behind and become a homebody, as well as for every woman who still has to fit her home management skills in between busy away from home workdays, hoping to one day leave that *"other job"* behind. In today's depressed high-unemployment economy more and more women are finding themselves at home again quite unexpectedly, and trying to learn how to adjust to being full-time homemakers. This book is written for the homemaker who wants to go beyond surviving to thriving--at home, for good!

* <u>Find Your Strongest Life: What the Happiest and Most Successful Women Do Differently</u> by Marcus Buckingham (Thomas Nelson, Inc. 2009)

— 1 —

WHAT IS A HOMEMAKER?

It's an exuberant spring day, and I'm knee deep in the process of transplanting lilies in our back yard. My hair is askew, my sweatshirt is sweaty, and my sneakers are caked with mud as I labor at digging another hole. In short, I am enjoying myself immensely.

My neighbor Ted approaches with clippers in hand and leans over the hedge. *"Hello, neighbor! How did you all survive the winter?"*

"Just great!" I reply, feeling as sunny as the moment.

"So how is the job going?"

"Oh, didn't you know? I quit my job."

"Oh. Really? Are you looking for a better one instead?" Ted asks nosily as he mops his brow.

My mind flashes back to the day Ted boasted about his wife receiving an award for five years at work without missing a day, and I wish he would drop the whole subject. I begin digging harder.

"Nope."

"Well, then, you must be selling real estate again."

"Nope," I repeat, digging furiously.

"Oh." (Pregnant pause.) *"Just what are you doing with yourself these days?"*

I wish I could throw Ted into this hole and quickly cover it over. I visualize myself jumping up and down on top of the mound of dirt as he muffles, *"You're doing whaaat?"*

Ted waits persistently for my answer. I shrug my shoulders and nervously giggle, *"Oh, I'm just a housewife!"*

Ted assumes a quizzical expression and mumbles something inane like, *"Oh . . . how interesting,"* before disappearing behind the shrubs. I resist the urge to lob a dirt clod at the back of his head. Suddenly the sky seems overcast, and I retreat to the hammock to berate myself.

What's the matter with me, anyway? Why do I feel so defensive every time someone asks me what I *"do"*? Ever since I decided to be a full-time homemaker, it's as if I'm afraid that others think I no longer qualify as a productive member of society. And why on earth did I say, *"I'm just a housewife"*?

Gardening forgotten, I gaze listlessly at the oak trees towering overhead and wonder what would be a good answer the next time someone asks me what I *"do"* now. Just what, exactly, is a homemaker anyway? I ask myself. I promptly decide that a homemaker is definitely not *"just a housewife."* That expression is so condescending—as if it is something one does only if she is incapable of doing anything else. It sounds like *"just breathing"* or *"just hanging around, doing nothing."* And I don't like the word *"housewife."* It sounds like someone married to her house. Yes, I decide, *"homemaker"* is a much better word than *"housewife."*

But just what is a homemaker?

She obviously is not considered by most people to be a career woman, even if homemaking is definitely her career of choice. And she hasn't the prestige of dashing off to her *"liberated career in the economic opportunity sphere,"* the status of an impressive title, nor even the reward of receiving a paycheck at the end of the week.

But the homemaker does have the satisfaction of knowing that what she does is much more valuable than any of those things—and it's far more rewarding in the long run. And she feels very important, even if her *"status"* is only appreciated by her family.

The career homemaker is also the definition of the word *"liberated"*—much more than any women's lib activists give her credit. She's relieved to be liberated from strident, unfeminine *"feminism"*---free to be as caring, nurturing, and gentle as she may wish to be. She is thankful to be liberated from the tyranny of the time clock, demands from department heads, and the time pressures of trying to handle a forty-plus hour a week job in addition to the jobs that never go away when one is a wife and mother. This sets her free to be her own boss, to schedule her own time, and to sleep late or even to take the day off if she chooses.

The homemaker is also liberated from the no-win situations that inevitably arise from trying to force a husband and children to do the tasks of a wife and mother while she is out trying to do a husband's job of providing for her family. She knows that not even a large corporation like Microsoft could survive if the company president, the software specialists, the administrative assistants, the janitors, and all the other employees were forced to do *"their share"* of everyone else's work. Every successful institution knows there is good reason for clear divisions of labor and definite job descriptions. The homemaker is happy to function solely in her role as wife, mother, and home manager. This frees her husband to concentrate fully on providing for his family. And it saves their children from an imposed, premature adulthood so they can *"just be kids"*. When their youngsters do grow up, they will be prepared to function as mature adults rather than overgrown, unfulfilled children who never got to experience a real childhood. Yes, the homemaker and her family are all very liberated.

Recent scientific studies have come to the conclusion that couples who split housework 50:50 are 50% more likely to split up! "*The more a man does in the home, the higher the divorce rate.*" Thomas Hansen, co-author of the 2012 study titled <u>Equality in the Home</u>. Surely having a homemaker can make for happier marriages.

One man commenting about that study wrote on-line in Mail Online News, "*It works extremely well for my wife and I, and also my happily married parents of 50 years. As a couple my wife and I have very defined roles, my job is to put a roof over our head, feed and clothe. My wife's job is to choose what roof, which food and clothes we wear. She and our son are my absolute number one priority and I work seven days a week to provide for them, my wife's priorities are myself and our son. The key to a good marriage is to put your other half first."*

THE HOMEMAKER DEFINED

Even though a full-time, stay-at-home wife and mother grows more scarce with every decade, she is not, as many would have us believe, a relic of a bygone era, a Wilma Flintstone, or even a June Cleaver. Nor is she a spoiled *"princess"* who idles away the hours while the maid does all the work. Her husband can be the king of his castle because that makes her the queen. She is content to be her husband's helpmeet as well as his cheerleader, his comforter, and his primary ally against a difficult and sometimes degrading world. She does not compete with her husband, but complements him. Even though they may in many ways be opposites, together they balance one another, and function as a strong united *"one"*.

In this era of expected two-paycheck families, she appreciates having a husband who supports her stay-at-home career. He, in turn, is thankful to have a wife who chooses to make homemaking her primary, rather than secondary, concern. He knows that after expenses incurred from child care, transportation, work-related clothes, and eating out, the average American woman nets very little in exchange for the strain placed upon her and the rest of the family. He considers a more frugal lifestyle well worth the true higher standard of living his family enjoys as the result of having a wife dedicated to managing their home lovingly, wisely, and more economically. Most of all, he enjoys having a wife who has the time and energy to devote to being his friend and lover.

The career homemaker and her husband are not easily fooled into believing the trite truisms that are accepted without question by society today, such as,

"You just can't live on one paycheck anymore," and *"Families can't afford to have women in the home like they did in the past."* Granted, they can't always do it and still live a higher standard of living than their parents and grandparents did. But if they are willing to live as frugally and wisely as their grandparents did today's couples can live happy, successful lives with Mom at home.

They know that most couples today are just not content to live as simply as earlier generations did, who did not spend precious income on the things we consider *"necessities"* that we do now such as cable TV, cell phones for every family member, cars for every teenager, video games, sporting and entertainment events, and more and more *"stuff"*. Compare the size of our homes, the clothes in our closets, the options on our cars, and our staggering credit card debt to those of earlier generations. If the homemaker must choose between the pursuit of insatiable materialism or the pursuit of a homemaking career, the homemaker agrees that *"godliness actually is a means of great gain, when accompanied by contentment"* (1 Timothy 6:6). Or as the ancient philosopher Euripides put it, *"Enough is abundance to the wise."*

The homemaker does not, however, judge those who feel otherwise. She has sincere compassion for those women who have no other recourse than an outside-the-home job. She has no desire to add to their burden with criticism. Instead, she often cares for their children and offers a kind hand wherever she can help. Most of us have *"been there; done that,"* and know how hard it is to try to do it all.

The career homemaker is also a devoted mother. Whether her children are very young or have left the nest, they know that Mom is always there for them at a moment's notice. The homemaker never ceases to be a mother. At various stages of her life, her kids may ask, *"Mommy, did I tell you that I have to be a frog in the school play tomorrow?"* or *"Mama, do you think I have a fever?"* or *"Hey, Mom, we need a babysitter— what are you doing Saturday night?"* She enjoys listening to, caring for, and teaching her children. She will never have to say, like Roseanne Barr once joked, *"I'm the mother they never had."*

The homemaker considers her children to be her greatest treasures, and she endeavors to raise them accordingly. She doesn't entrust their upbringing to the school, the state, or to paid surrogate mothers. As a result, her children benefit from enjoying not only quality time but quantity time with their mother.

The career homemaker does not concern herself with whether or not her duties are all *"fun."* She doesn't kid herself: changing diapers and cleaning toilets is not all laughs. But she understands that fun does not equal happiness. She knows that fun is the feeling one derives from a temporary enjoyable act, like gliding down a water slide or floating along in a hot air balloon. But happiness is the feeling one has between all those few and fleeting fun moments. If fun could make a person happy, she concludes, then why is the world full of so many laughing, partying, fun-loving people who are living hollow, depressed and debt-ridden lives?

The maxim *"No pain, no gain,"* applies not only to the physical conditioning of our bodies but to life in general. The homemaker knows that everything capable of bringing real happiness also comes at a price. She considers marriage, childbirth, motherhood, spiritual growth, and homemaking all to be pursuits worthy of their cost. She doesn't expect every moment to be fun, but she does expect her efforts to bring happiness—and they do.

A homemaker is also a very adaptable person. She must function under pressure in an overwhelming variety of roles: chauffeur, nutritionist, nurse, counselor, teacher, social secretary, financial director, interior decorator, savvy bargain hunter, holiday planner and entertainer, good neighbor and informed citizen, church volunteer, scout leader, and disaster relief worker. She attempts to do all that and more with an air of grace, always striving to be the best person that she can be in the process. No one is harder on her than herself when she fails. Thankfully, the homemaker is also resilient!

The career homemaker knows that the only way that she can accomplish the many demands made on her is to be an excellent organizer and time manager. If she *"just can't get everything done"* and is suffering pressure from time constraints, her anxiety may be caused by two things. First, she may not be using her time wisely. Second, she may be suffering from the *"Supermom Syndrome"*—trying to be all things to all people and putting unnecessary expectations upon herself. Ninety percent of the time her frustration stems from the latter cause.

To avoid these problems the homemaker can do several things. First, she can start her day whenever possible with a *"quiet time"* in which she seeks God's guidance and wisdom for that day. She knows that He will not give her more things to do in one day than she has the hours in which to do them. She does not over-schedule her time, but she allows God the freedom to add to or delete from her schedule as He chooses. And she does not create self-imposed guilt by setting higher standards for herself than God has asked her to set. She lives her life according to the Bible's standards, rather than Martha Stewart's--which are quite different!

Also, the homemaker strives to be organized. She prioritizes her time; she organizes her home for greater efficiency; and she eliminates the non-essentials. In her personal life as well as in her home she considers clutter to be her enemy and simplicity to be her friend.

The successful homemaker does not waste time. She considers her time on this earth to be a finite gift from God, and she does not squander it on foolish TV shows, trashy romance novels, or long telephone gossip sessions. She does not say yes to anything she is not absolutely sure she wants to do. And she knows that *if she has time for tennis, bridge, garden club, or even church activities but does not have time to manage her home wisely, then her priorities are out of order.*

The homemaker uses her time wisely so that she can also pursue activities that are important to her personal rejuvenation. She considers time spent on herself, including relaxing and enjoying her solitary

13

company, to be time well spent. She insists on having time with her husband and with her children. And she enjoys having time to practice the nearly extinct art of hospitality. She knows that the only way she can enjoy these pleasant activities is to guard her time like the treasure that it is, and manage it wisely. Every minute she wastes is a minute she has lost to spend as she wishes.

A Christian homemaker also honors the Word of God. Scripture tells her that *"older women likewise are to ... encourage the young women to love their husbands, to love their children, to be sensible, pure, workers at home ... that the word of God may not be dishonored"* (Titus 2:3-5). As a sincere disciple of Christ, she does not consider obedience to the word of God to be optional.

She seeks to pattern herself after the godly women throughout the Scriptures, such as the excellent wife described in Proverbs 31. Like that homemaker, she strives to be productive, kind, wise, and such a blessing to her husband and children that they have *"no lack of gain"* because of her constant vigilance on their behalf.

But, most of all, the homemaker attempts to pattern herself after Jesus himself, who embodied what it means to be a servant, comforter, healer, peacemaker, teacher, lover of little children, and giver of life. All that she does, no matter how seemingly insignificant, she does most of all for Him. And she strives to do all things as Jesus does them—motivated by love, in perfect order and subjection to the Father, with grace and beauty.

Being a successful homemaker requires a very emotionally mature and wise woman. Becoming one is a process of self-discovery and growth that never ends, even after her children have left the nest.

Brother Lawrence, the humble seventeenth century monk and author of <u>The Practice of the Presence of God</u> was *"happy to pick up a straw from the ground just for the love of God."* In that same way, the homemaker is pleased to do the humblest of tasks. Whether she is making a bed or wiping a little nose, when she remembers for whom she is really doing it, she derives a great sense of contentment and purpose.

14

What is a homemaker? In short, she is a person who makes a home. To her, a home must be more than just a bed and fast-food stop. *Just as she recognizes that the family is the strength of a nation, she knows that the home is the strength of the family.* She strives to make her home a place of beauty, order, and security—a positive retreat from a negative and turbulent world. There her family finds the healing and renewal they need to face that world anew each day. There they are healed and built up, rather than broken and beaten down. There they can be open and vulnerable, knowing they are loved unconditionally.

That is the home this homemaker strives to create, realizing that she is has a crucial role in the overall atmosphere of her home. She sets the standards, for excellence or not, for contentment or not, and for love—or not. The homemaker strives to make her home a garden where love can grow between her and her husband, free of the weeds of contention and criticism. Her home is a greenhouse for tender, growing children. And she is the gardener. That, I decide, is what a homemaker is.

Then I pick up my shovel and begin to plant lilies.

── 2 ──

NEVER CLEAN FOR COMPANY

"Sometimes I think about just quitting my job and staying home," my friend Evelyn confided over lunch. *"I get tired of the same old nine-to-five routine. I can afford to quit if I really want to. But when I get right down to doing it, I lose my nerve. You see,"* she added pensively, *"I'm just not the type to stay home and clean house all day."*

Many women consider homemaking to be synonymous with only one thing—cleaning the house. No wonder so many women are reluctant to be career homemakers. They have entered the job market by the droves because even the hassles of a job look glamorous compared to keeping company with Mr. Clean. And if cleaning house is all there is to homemaking, who can blame them?

That's how Jacky felt, too. Despite having three active children, a beautiful house, and a husband who provided well for the family, she was dissatisfied with her life at home.

"I'm too intelligent to waste my life behind a mop and broom," she complained. *"I hate housework. I'm not good at it, either. I'd rather do anything else."*

So Jacky got a job. And who does the housework in Jacky's home now? Her husband does. And when does he do all that housework? On Saturdays. Jacky

17

abandoned homemaking to escape doing what her husband accomplishes on his day off. It makes me wonder.

I also wonder about people like Pat. She's a full-time homemaker who makes herself miserable over housework. She never seems to get caught up. Whenever you go to her house, she makes you uncomfortable by apologizing profusely for *"this awful mess."* She acts as if you came to inspect her home, not to enjoy her company. She seems to be in constant anguish over what she thinks is an insurmountable task—getting the house clean.

Pat has an especially hard time whenever she is expecting house guests. She works herself into a frenzy, trying to accomplish in one day what hasn't been done in months. By the time her guests arrive, Pat is too exhausted to be much of a hostess. She simply horrifies them by looking so haggard and telling them how very hard she worked to prepare for their visit. Her guests then feel guilty for putting her through all that work. It's a no-win situation.

If only Pat knew that she should never clean for company. It really shouldn't be necessary. With just a little organization and discipline, Pat could make sure her house looks good enough for company *all the time*. No extra fuss. No last minute panic. Pat could invest all that wasted energy she spends on worry, rationalization, and procrastination on one four hour cleaning session per week, or less. And she could maintain that clean appearance in only thirty minutes a day. The rest of her week would be free to pursue other interests.

If women like Pat, Jacky and Evelyn understood that homemaking is much more than just cleaning the house perhaps they would begin to enjoy the great rewards of a homemaking career. Of course, homemaking includes housework. Cleanliness is a basic necessity for every home. No amount of fancy decorating can hide dirt. The successful homemaker must first provide a clean environment for the health of her family and herself.

And according to one study that I read American homemakers now expend 360 less calories per day than they did in 1965—explaining in large part why we have become, well, larger! The best (free!) way to slim down is to do more physical work in the home.

But some women act like cleaning is a dirty word. However housework, if done in an organized method, needs not be terribly time consuming. And it doesn't need to be a task that takes all of the joy out of being the manager of a home. Housework is one of those areas where an ounce of prevention is worth a pound of cure. A weekly cleaning routine keeps the work from piling up into an overwhelming chore. And a daily touch-up session keeps the house looking fresh all week.

HOW TO CLEAN LIKE A PRO

I, too, used to spend far too much time cleaning the house. But when our sons started school I took a part-time job and thought I no longer had time for all that housework. So I hired a housekeeper. She came once a week, and she was expensive. But she was worth it. I looked forward to coming home once a week to a sparkling, orderly house. It was such a luxury to know that someone had done all those hours of housework for me.

Then one summer I learned from the boys just how much time my housekeeper spent doing *"all those hours of housework."* I asked them to time how long she stayed while I was away at work. Their observation was that she was there barely more than two hours! I couldn't believe it! I had them time her the next week, and the next. But she consistently accomplished in only two hours what it had always taken me much longer to do. This startling revelation led me to ask myself three serious questions:

How could she clean my house in only two hours?
If she could clean my house in only two hours, why couldn't I?
If I could clean my house in only two hours, why was I paying her to do it?

That's when I decided to revolutionize my method of cleaning the house! I decided to stop cleaning like I had all week to do it and start cleaning like a professional. A professional cleans as quickly and efficiently as possible, treating housework like a business, not a hobby. So my goal became doing the best job in the least amount of time. But, for the sake of doing a good job without unnecessary time pressure, I decided to allow myself twice as much time as my housekeeper took—up to four hours.

Then I broke down my housework duties into just four categories:

- Dust
- Clean Floors
- Clean the kitchen
- Clean the bathrooms

This allowed me one hour to do each of these four jobs. But could I do it? After my first trial run I learned it was not only possible, but easy. Here's how you can do it, too:

Choose one morning or afternoon per week for your housework, and stick to that schedule if possible. Write it on your calendar so you won't inadvertently plan something else during that time. Make it a weekly appointment, and soon it will become a regular habit. *Or*, instead, choose one hour per day, Monday through Thursday, and just spend that hour on one of the areas to clean that day. That is what I do now that I am home full-time.

I like to clean the house early in the week. Weekends are the messiest time of the week, so a good cleaning early in the week seems to last longer than if I cleaned on Friday. I would never clean on Friday anyway because like to make Fridays my *"errand day"* for shopping, etc. And make it a rule from now on to never clean house on the same day you're having company!

My friend Barb said, *"That's fine if you don't have preschoolers at home, but I do. There's just too much constant clutter all over the house from the children for me to make any headway on cleaning."* I suggested that Barb try the solution that I found to that problem when my boys were home all day. I removed all the toys from their bedrooms except for their stuffed animals and books. The toys went down to our unfinished basement where I put them in toy boxes and on shelves. There they had plenty of room to ride their tricycles and run off steam on cold or rainy days, and an area rug on which to sit and scatter toys to their hearts' delight. But if they wanted to play with their toys upstairs, they were allowed to bring up only one thing at a time, and it had to be taken back downstairs before they could bring up another toy. It worked wonderfully, allowing the children the freedom to make their own choices in what they wanted to do while teaching them to pick up after themselves, too.

If you aren't lucky enough to have a basement, you can arrange nice storage in the child's bedroom to organize all of their toys, and just allow them to take out one particular toy or basket of toys at a time. They need to put that away before pulling out something else. It helps with younger children to have the most cluttery, messy toys put up where they can't pull them out without supervision. Young children are simply overwhelmed by a roomful of piles of toys, just as you are, and cannot even begin to pick them up when done. Limiting the number of toys they can pull out at one time actually increases their contentment level.

Another alternative could be to work out a babysitting exchange with a neighbor; you watch her children while she cleans her house if she will keep your children while you clean yours. It's well worth the effort of setting up a schedule to allow the rest of your week to be free from worrying about housework.

A word of caution: The following simple tips can revolutionize your life. You'll never again have to fear an unexpected knock at the door. Company will always be welcome. You will know that your work is done, eliminating energy-sapping worry and guilt. Your time and energy will be free for more important and enjoyable things. And you might even find that you enjoy housework!

But, on the other hand, your new housework schedule must not become too important. If family or friends need you, of course, your schedule must have some flexibility. Just be sure you aren't using those opportunities for service to avoid your household tasks. If, however, you don't get everything done on schedule this week, there's always next week. It will wait for you, and you will get to it next time. This schedule, however you decide to set it up, is designed to *free* you—not to be master over you.

Do take care not to turn your home into a showroom unfit for human occupation. Your home, after all, is also your family's home—and they should feel *comfortable* there. Nobody else cares if your two-year-old has Legos scattered all over the family room floor, so why should you? And it's better to have several messy teenagers sprawled all over your house than who-knows-where-else.

If someone comes over in the midst of a bit of people-clutter like that, be confident enough not to apologize for the mess. This avoids the old arguments, *"Oh, it's not half as bad as my house,"* and *"No, your house is always cleaner than mine."* Just allow your guest to feel at ease because you are, whatever the state of your house. This is an important element to being a gracious hostess.

Being organized and capable of cleaning your house in four hours or less does not eliminate the need to teach your children how to do these things. Daughters should be taught how to do housework so that they will one day be capable of taking care of their own families. Sons should be taught how to do housework so they won't get married just because they don't know how to take care of themselves. Homemaking skills should be taught to children so they gradually gain self-sufficiency—not so they do our work for us. Heaven knows, it's easier to do it yourself than to take the time to teach our children how to do it.

Many women complain that housework is *"no-brain"* work, making it monotonous and boring. So they turn on the TV and get hooked on soap operas or other nonproductive programs. No wonder they call it a no-brainer. Think! Why not use your housework time productively instead? You can use it as time to invest in yourself. You can use it to learn. You can listen to audio books or iPod music collections that are inspiring, educational, or uplifting. Most libraries carry a great selection of free audio-books that you might otherwise never have the time to read. They also carry classical music that you can use to learn all about the works of Beethoven or Vivaldi. Or listen to the Bible on C.D. or a Christian teaching series. I enjoy talk radio while I work. And then of course there are all the free versions of books, music and teachings that you can download right off your computer onto your iPod or other listening device. You can even learn a language from teaching programs. I get so involved in some of these things that I finish my housework before I'm ready to stop listening. If I want to work quickly, I put on some upbeat music and dance through my work. (I'm glad no one can see me clogging to bluegrass while I dust!)

Have you ever complained that you just don't have enough time for prayer? If so, here's a great four-hour slot that can be used for that purpose. While your body is doing the physical work, your spirit can petition God for special needs, engage in spiritual warfare, or just lift up heavenly praises. If you use your time like that, you won't ever again complain that housework is boring. If you finish a particular job in less than an hour, stop! Then reward yourself and put your feet up for a few minutes while you sip a cup of tea. Make your work more fun by learning to give yourself little goals and rewards throughout the day.

If you wonder in what order to do your daily tasks each morning *before* starting your daily housework, a general guideline is to take care of things in this order:

1. **People:** Get yourself groomed and dressed for the day, then take care of the needs of the rest of the family and help get them off to school or work. (Don't send them off while you are looking scary!)
2. **Pets:** Feed and water the pets. Walk the dog. Brush the cat. Talk to the bird.
3. **Plants:** Water them; pick off the dead leaves, etc.

4. Projects: Do your 30 minute daily pick-up (see below.)

Then begin your scheduled daily task.

   Here's an example of a four-hour morning schedule if you prefer to do your entire house cleaning in one day:

8:00-9:00 a.m. Dust
9:00-10:00 a.m. Clean Floors
10:00-11:00 a.m. Clean the kitchen
11:00-noon Clean the bathrooms

Let's look at each cleaning chore in more detail.

DUST

You may wonder, *"Why should I dust first? Won't I just stir up more dust when I vacuum?"* You dust first for two reasons: First, dusting often knocks little bits of debris onto the floors. Second, many people have plush carpeting that shows footprints, so they prefer not to vacuum first and then track footprints all over the carpeting when dusting.

Vacuuming after you dust will not stir up dust if you take the following precautions. First, change your furnace filter as often as recommended to keep dust out of the air circulation. Buy enough filters at a time, so you'll only have to purchase them once a year. Buy them when they are on sale. Second, if you consistently clean your house once a week, it will gradually have less and less dust in it. I know one woman who says she needs to dust only once a month. Her house must really be clean! If regular cleaning doesn't help, you may need a furnace cleaning service to power-vac your ventilation ducts. And third, do have a vacuum that uses HEPA filters which capture nearly 100% of dust and allergens when you vacuum.

Starting at one end of the house, systematically dust one room at a time thoroughly. Dust from the top of the room to the bottom, from one side to the other.

Put away misplaced items and straighten the room as you work. Pick up small items rather than dusting around them. Use spray dusting liquid (or any good home recipe) and a clean rag (old fashioned unfolded type cloth diapers are my favorites) on flat surfaces and fingerprinted areas. If you carry along a damp rag and all-purpose spray cleaner you can swipe fingerprints from doors and woodwork as you go. I like to carry all my equipment in one large tote bag from room to room.

Purchasing a duster on a long handle is well worth the investment. I love the *"Swiffer"* brand duster with extendable handle. It will save you a lot of time and energy. You can use your duster to reach everything from ceiling fixtures to the baseboards. Use it to dust intricately carved crevices, caned chairs, window sills, and window blinds. Run it across your clean air return vents to keep dust from collecting there. A long handled duster makes dusting much easier, faster, and more thorough.

CLEAN THE FLOORS

During this hour you vacuum all the carpeting and mop or dust mop hardwood and tile floors, other than those in the kitchen and bathrooms. Sweep your front and back porch. And shake out the area throw rugs along the way.

Please do be kind enough to yourself to own a decent vacuum sweeper. Too often women exhaust themselves by pushing around a cheap imitation of a real sweeper because they're too *"frugal"* to invest in an effective cleaning machine. Men, however, rarely suffer from this particular martyr behavior. If they need a saw or a drill, they usually buy the deluxe model—even if they only need to use it once a year. How many men have elaborate carpentry machinery collecting cobwebs in their basements while their wives struggle upstairs behind a worn out, twenty-year-old cheap sweeper?

Once my friend Kim was vigorously pulling her old sweeper behind her and wondered why her little boy began to scream, " *'Moke! 'Moke!"* as he excitedly pointed at the sweeper. She turned around to see that black smoke was pouring out of it!

So don't skimp on having a safe, powerful sweeper that does the work for you, instead of making you do it. Today they aren't prohibitively expensive (at least compared to the latest power saws), and they even save you money by cleaning your carpeting better and prolonging its life. And, of course, a HEPA filter vac is a real necessity to keep allergens from attacking your family, or a sealed type of sweeper system, like our central vac, that keeps dust from escaping.

Sweep systematically and thoroughly from one room to the next. Don't wear yourself out by trying to sweep under every piece of furniture every week—nobody but the cat walks under there anyway. Just concentrate on doing an extra thorough job on a different room each week, and you'll never be overwhelmed by needing to do it all at once.

If you have a convenient place to store one, it's also nice to have a little quickie vac to pull out for crumbs and tracked spots during the week. It's a lot easier than lugging out a big sweeper for a little job. There are even vacuuming robots, like my *"Mint"* brand little helper, which I named *"Bob"*, and who is great for daily touch-ups on non-carpeted floors. My friend bought a small floor-and-carpet type of floorbot. They don't do a thorough job like a larger vacuum, but they are great for everyday touch-ups—especially if you have pet hair issues.

CLEAN THE KITCHEN

Shake out throw rugs and set them aside. Mop the floor with a household floor cleaning solution appropriate for your type of flooring. Right now I am a *"Swiffer"* brand mop addict—I love using the wet wipes to mop the floors.

Once the floor is clean, fill the sink with cleanser and wipe off all the countertops and appliances. Soak dirty stove drip pans in the water while you work, then wash them off and replace them. Get as much clutter off the countertops and top of the refrigerator as possible. Too many magnets and clippings on the front of the refrigerator can make the whole kitchen look messy. If you have a lot of paper clutter, put up a bulletin board, or better yet use a file folder system on your desktop. When you're finished, just replace the rugs and put an attractive centerpiece on the table. The kitchen looks and smells great!

CLEAN THE BATHROOM

You can clean a bathroom well in approximately twenty to thirty minutes, allowing you to clean two or three bathrooms in an hour. Remove everything that you can from the bathroom and place it all on a throw rug or towel on the floor outside the bathroom. You don't want to be cleaning around soap dishes and knick-knacks.

In a plastic bucket, basket, or wastebasket, make a bathroom cleaning kit consisting of a can (I prefer the *"Scrubbing Bubbles"* or similar brand) of your favorite cleanser, a spray bottle of window cleaner like *"Windex"* or even your own mixture of vinegar and water, rubber gloves, and clean rags.

Anything other than that is probably not necessary—including cute little plastic mushroom shaped deodorizers and blue toilet water dyes. *A clean room always smells good.* All your bathroom needs to look and smell great is a good cleaning and a fat cake of fresh soap in the soap dish. Don't be fooled into buying lots of expensive cleansers and deodorizers that you don't need. You can spend that money on scented soaps or luxurious bubble bath instead if you wish.

Clean bath fixtures in the following order: sink, tub and then the toilet. Wash the floor last with a separate clean rag or mop. This prevents spreading bacterial contamination from dirty areas to less dirty areas. To make rinsing the shower and tub walls easier, you may want to install a shower head on a hose extension. You'll eliminate the *"drippy elbow syndrome"* forever.

Clean the mirror and polish the chrome fixtures to a shine with window spray. Then shake out the throw rugs, empty the wastebasket, and throw dirty towels in the washing machine. You can turn on the washing machine and get all the towels washed right then and there. Return everything to its place, and you're done.

Now fill up the tub with some warm water, pour in some of that fancy scented bubble bath that you bought, and jump in for a long soak. It's only noon, and your whole house is clean for the week! Once you get your four-hour routine down to a science, you may want to start by stripping the beds and keeping the washer and dryer running while you work. You can have all the bedding and towels washed and back in place by the time your work is done.

DAILY MAINTENANCE WALK-THROUGH

No house is going to stay spotless all week if it has people living in it, so a little daily maintenance is necessary. That's why a thirty-minute touch-up session every morning means the difference between a house that looks like you cleaned it recently and a house that looks like you cleaned it today. Plan your touch-up session after the family has left for work and school, and after you've gotten dressed for the day. It's important to do this every morning. Once it becomes a daily habit you won't know how you ever lived any other way:

1. **Make your bed.** Who wants to crawl into a wrinkled, unmade bed at night? (No one!) Have you ever faced that depressing situation, only to make the bed before crawling into it? So why not just make the bed first thing in the morning, so you don't have to look at it all day? Kathy used to think that she didn't have time to make her bed on very rushed days. Then I challenged her to time herself. She was shocked; it took just three minutes. Now she knows that she can always spare three minutes to make her bed. When you first get out of bed, throw back to covers to *"air out"* the bed for at least ten minutes. This actually kills dust mites by

exposing them to light, as well as freshening up the linens. Straighten your bedroom, putting away clothes, books, etc. Open the curtains and let the sunshine in. Sunshine kills dust mites and germs!

2. **Check each child's room.** Teach them to make their own beds and put away their own clothes and toys. Supervise the little ones pleasantly so they will have a positive attitude about caring for their own room.

3. **Straighten the bathrooms.** Throw dirty towels in the hamper and close the shower curtain to prevent mildew between the folds (or buy mildew-resistant curtains). Keep a bottle of window cleaner under the sink so you can spray and wipe the mirror and vanity top. The bathroom will look and smell like you just cleaned the whole room. This is probably the single most important work saver you can perform. Try it!

4. **Walk through the remaining rooms** of the house. As you go through each one, straighten and put away clutter. You may want to carry a basket with you for carrying things from one room to the next. This takes very little time but makes an enormous difference.

5. **Straighten the kitchen last.** Put away breakfast dishes and wipe off countertops and table. Pull from the freezer whatever you plan to cook for dinner, or get the crock pot going if you plan to be away all day. If you're the only one home during the day, you may want to set the dinner table now, saving yourself precious moments at the hectic dinner hour. You'll thank yourself at 6:00 p.m. for everything you do now.

6. **Throw a load of clothes in the washing machine and turn it on.** You can throw them in the dryer at dinner time and fold them after doing the dishes. Doing a load a day like this

keeps laundry day from becoming a huge task. I do laundry throughout the week during my cleaning time, and don't really need a laundry day anymore. My husband's dress shirts go to the dry cleaners, and very little else needs a touch-up with today's wash and wear fabrics.

Keeping this touch-up routine as a daily habit is the greatest secret to being an organized, efficient housekeeper. For the few minutes a day it requires, it's more than worth the freedom and self-esteem it pays in return. Soon you'll find your friends asking you how on earth you do it all. You can even tell them your secret if you want to. (But you don't have to!)

ACTION ASSIGNMENTS

- *Time how long it takes you to make your bed.*
- *Time how long it takes you to do each of the four categories of housecleaning: dusting, vacuuming, bathrooms, and kitchen. Can you do each one in an hour or less?*
- *Assign yourself a time to do your weekly housecleaning and write it on your calendar-- either in one four hour block, or one hour per day. See if you can accomplish it in four hours or less—and in the time slot that you scheduled.*
- *Plan what mentally productive thing you will do while cleaning your house (such as listening to books or praying). See if you feel that it makes your work more enjoyable.*
- *Make a cleaning kit to keep in one of your bathrooms for your weekly cleaning. Put a pair of plastic gloves, a bottle of cleanser, a bottle of window spray cleaner, and some clean rags in an easy to carry container. Put another bottle of window spray in each of your other bathrooms for the thirty-minute daily touch-up.*
- *Make a note on your calendar for when to change your furnace/air conditioner. Make note of your filter size in your organizer and buy a year's worth when they are on sale.*

3

NO MORE SPRING CLEANING

Our grandmothers had an annual ritual that came as surely as crocus, daffodils, and little green apples. They called it *"spring cleaning"*--that wildly disruptive time of year when all other activities ceased so that everything could be cleaned that hadn't been cleaned since the year before. Families fled for the outdoors to escape the commotion as Grandma furiously shook out carpets, washed windows, and scrubbed everything else to a spit shine. In the process Grandma also wore herself to a frazzle. Fortunately, spring cleaning only came once a year—and Grandma needed that long to rest up from it.

Today not many women have the time and energy to invest in an annual spring cleaning. We have schedules far too crammed full of carpooling, shopping, and attending soccer games to allow us a couple of weeks devoted exclusively to deep-cleaning our homes every spring.

So what happens to our homes if they never get the benefit of that old-fashioned spring cleaning? Do we try, unsuccessfully and halfheartedly, to fit it in here and there? Do we decide to ignore the gray fuzz on the top edge of the drapes until we buy new ones? Do we search the Yellow Pages for someone who advertises, *"We do windows, wash and iron curtains, and pick the grit out of your sliding glass door tracks"?* (Lotsa luck!) Or do we just forget about it until it's our turn to have the family over for Thanksgiving—and we find ourselves polishing the silver, ironing the good tablecloth, and cleaning out the china cabinet while trying to make the turkey and dressing? What else can a busy homemaker do?

The best method I've found to keep my home in decent condition while avoiding a yearly *"spring cleaning"* is simple—just do the work in smaller bits throughout the year. Instead of consolidating all your deep cleaning into one or two exhausting weeks, break the work down into twelve segments—one segment for each month of the year.

For example, perhaps you would like to *"spring clean"* each room of the house once a year. Assign a room or special activity for each month of the year. A once-a-year deep cleaning is usually adequate for most areas if you practice the regular housecleaning described in Chapter 2. You may want to leave the month of December free of heavy housework and devote it to baking cookies, mailing Christmas cards, and doing last-minute shopping. On a piece of paper list your monthly special projects. When you finish, your list may look something like this:

January	Office and Files
February	Basement and/or Attic
March	Kitchen
April	Master bedroom and closet
May	Bedroom #2
June	Bedroom #3
July	Family room
August	Laundry room
September	Bathroom and linen closet
October	Living room, entry hall, coat closet

November   Dining room

December   Christmas activities

"But when during the month do I do all this cleaning?" you ask. One option is to spend some extra time on that particular area during your weekly cleaning routine. If it's the month to clean your bedroom, you might wash the curtains and clean the windows one week, clean out your closet and dresser drawers the next week, the third week you can wash the mattress pad and turn the mattress, and the last week of the month you could wipe down the walls and woodwork. You do as much of those extra things as you want to do each week. At the beginning of the next month, you start doing the same type of thing on the next project. Adding this extra work on the same day that you clean the whole house will mean you need another 30 minutes or so. But it's still easier than trying to do it all at one time of the year. And better than never doing it at all.

Another option, which I prefer, is to schedule yourself a Special Projects Day each week. Perhaps you choose Friday mornings. That's your morning to do all the *"spring cleaning"* you want on your monthly project. If you don't finish that week, you follow up with more work the next week, and the next, until you've accomplished all you want to on that particular project. This method gives you time to do a much more thorough job. You can even tackle extra fixing-up or decorating projects on that room as well.

Sometimes I get my monthly Special Project done in one morning, and sometimes it takes *"a month of Fridays."* Sometimes the room just needs a good cleaning. Other times I may decide to paint the woodwork, make new curtains, or rearrange all the furniture. Regardless of how much or how little I do, *my goal is to feel good about that room at the end of the month.*

Keep in mind that Special Projects Day is your once-a-year opportunity to take a good, hard look at each room and reassess its appearance and function. *Look at that room as if you were a guest seeing it for the first time.* We can get so accustomed to our surroundings that we no longer realize how they look to others. We may not notice the little fingerprints accumulating on the door frames. We may not see that the sofa needs a good upholstery scrubbing. Maybe the kitchen curtain over the sink has grown faded and worn. Perhaps you never noticed that heavy traffic is wearing a path in the carpeting in front of the sofa. Use this time to view your home through a more critical eye.

It's amazing how we can overlook the obvious through habit. When I sold real estate, our office took weekly tours of pre-owned homes that had just been placed on the market. Some of the homes were very attractive and well-maintained. But most of those homes were, at best, dull and neglected. Some were even disgracefully dark, cluttered and filthy. I wondered if the people trying to sell their homes ever really looked at what they had grown accustomed to living in.

After I put someone's home on the market, the owners often began to hurriedly *"fix it up"* to attract a buyer. They rushed to paint, repair, and replace things that had needed their attention for years. Now that they were moving out of the house, they were getting all that done. But they could have enjoyed the fruits of their own efforts had they only done it when their home first needed repair. Now they were doing it for someone else—and doing it under pressure. What a waste!

Remember that nothing you do to keep your home well-maintained is a waste. It always adds to the value of your home as well as your present enjoyment of it. A well-maintained home is much more peaceful. Your home is your most valuable investment, so it doesn't pay to neglect it. Postponed maintenance costs more in the long run. Having a Special Projects routine is one way to be sure your home is always in excellent condition and *"market ready"* if you should suddenly need to move.

Here are some suggestions for your Special Projects activities:

SUGGESTIONS FOR EVERY ROOM

Write down projects that you need to do or items that you need to buy. As you work you may notice that you need more hangers, shelf paper, or baskets for organizing small items. If you don't write it down when you think of it, you probably won't remember it when you go to the store.

Repair anything that is broken. Tighten wiggly doorknobs and switch plates. (Yes, you can do this yourself!) Re-glue curling edges of wallpaper. Put plastic wallpaper guards on corners to prevent wear. Replace burned-out light bulbs and wash light fixtures. Clean or replace dirty lamp shades. Have damaged windows or screens repaired. Touch up wooden furniture with scratch remover.

Clean windows and window treatments. Take draperies to the cleaners, or just air them out on the clothesline or in the dryer on *"Cool Air."* Launder curtains.

Wipe down all walls. Use a weak solution of mild ammonia and water to remove visible dirt and invisible mold and pollens. Remove pictures and plaques from the walls as you wash them. Wear rubber gloves and be careful not to cut your hand on exposed nails, as I once did. Wash baseboards, doors, door frames, and window frames. You may decide to paint if just washing doesn't liven the room.

Clean the floors. Shampoo carpeting. Wash throw rugs. Strip and re-wax wood or linoleum floors if needed.

Redecorate dull rooms as your budget allows. Perhaps it's time to recover the sofa or replace that worn rug. Maybe you want to make a new tablecloth and curtains out of a couple of sheets you found on sale. If you enjoy crafts, make a new flower arrangement or wall hanging. Crochet a pretty afghan for that bare rocker sitting in the corner. Not all redecorating has to be expensive, and small touches can really brighten a room. Children's' bed sheets make great new curtains. Just line them with a plain sheet.

Re-arrange what you already have. It's amazing how moving the furniture or grouping some pictures on the wall can achieve dramatic results. Try to group similar objects in one place, such as all your figurines or your collection of pill boxes. Collections and vignettes are so much better than scattered isolated pieces, which amount to clutter. Place furniture in a more practical, use-oriented arrangement, such as making an entertainment area near the stereo and TV. Design a quiet area for reading or table games. This is your chance to use your dormant creativity. Pretend that you are *"staging"* a room, like realtors do, to sell your home. You really can make a room look like new without spending a cent.

Eliminate clutter. Clutter is your enemy! Simplicity is your friend! They cannot co-habit. Search out the clutter in your home and eliminate it. Many people live under the false impression that beauty comes from the over-accumulation of things. We need to take the oriental attitude that beauty comes from a proper balance between occupied and empty space. I once read that *"simplicity, taken to the extreme, becomes elegance."* Allow your home to have the elegance of graceful, peaceful spaces.

Take a lesson from the decorators of display homes. By using only the absolute minimum of items needed to make each room functional and attractive, they create beauty and spaciousness. Begin by seeing how much you can eliminate from each room in your house. (Yes, you can store it in the basement until you're sure this is what you want to do.)

Most homes have too many pieces of furniture crowding the floors, too many pictures and plaques hanging on the walls, and too many knick-knacks crammed onto tabletops and shelves. Even our garages become so stuffed that we can no longer park our cars in them. Society's answer is to have bigger closets, more shelves and cabinets, and larger homes. As author Richard Foster puts it, *"It is time to awaken to the fact that conformity to a sick society is to be sick."* The more sane approach is to remove as many of our nonessentials as possible and allow each room to breathe. Our goal should be to see how little, rather than how much, we can be happy with.

One way to prevent overcrowding is to allow how much space you have tell you how much you should own. Small closets means having fewer clothes—just be much more particular about the clothes you have. Most people only wear 20% of their clothes anyway. Smaller rooms mean less furniture. A smaller kitchen means fewer dishes and gadgets. We really can live with that much more easily than the stress of cramming and piling and overcrowding.

The big bonus of eliminating clutter is that the less you have in each room, the easier its upkeep becomes. Living by the *"Less is More"* motto conserves money, time, and energy. As every backpacker knows, the lighter the load, the more enjoyable the trip. Many Christians have shirked their obligation to be the salt of the earth and the light of the world because they're too busy with the maintenance of their possessions. We become indistinguishable from the world in our collecting and comparing.

The pursuit of more things ultimately drives us from our homemaking careers. We spend time earning the money to buy our possessions, then we spend time shopping for them, then we must invest precious hours in cleaning, repairing, and maintaining them. Remember that anything you own also, in turn, owns a piece of you. The less our possessions encumber us, the more we can allow God to own us. Can we have a better motivation to eliminate clutter?

Reorganize everything that you decide to keep. Store things where you'll use them. Group similar items together. Bring order to your possessions as you deep clean each room in your home. Put similar items together to form an interesting collection, rather than in cluttery bits and pieces throughout the house. Our God is a God of order. Order reflects His presence in our homes and in our lives. And it sure makes things a whole lot easier to find.

SUGGESTIONS FOR THE BATHROOM

Install a separate towel bar or hook for each member of the family, assigning one to each person. Instruct them to hang their wet towels there after bathing. There is no reason a bath towel can't be used more than once by the same person, saving you the equivalent of one mountain of laundry per week, not to mention a lot of wasted laundry soap and water. A couple of times each week gather all the towels and throw them into the wash during your thirty-minute touch-up time. After they're dry, re-hang them on their towel bars. This eliminates time wasted on folding and putting them away.

Purchase a small plastic crate or wicker basket for each family member to store his or her personal toiletries under the sink or on a shelf. If space is a problem, make a rule that one basket per person is the limit.

Eliminate bathroom quarrels by purchasing a tube of toothpaste for each family member to keep in his or her basket. Then anyone can squeeze in the middle or leave the cap off without upsetting those who prefer to do it differently.

Keep your own cosmetics and skin care products to a minimum to save space and money. Nobody needs 37 different shades of lipstick, eye shadow, and nail polish! Display them in a pretty basket or on a cosmetics tray. Keep it neat and clean. Few things are less attractive than a drippy, oozing make-up mess.

Store toweling neatly folded under the vanity or on wicker shelving where it can double as part of your room decor. Throw those ugly, shredding towels into the rag box and use your pretty ones. Don't be like my friend's grandmother who stored away her prettiest linens in a chest to pass on to future generations. When she passed away her children couldn't bear to use the things that she had denied herself, so they gave them all away.

Give each family member a personal clothes hamper for his or her room. Just remember that if it has a lid on it, they won't use it. Tell them to throw their clothes in their own hamper instead dropping them in the bathroom.

Keep bathroom decorations to a minimum to avoid clutter and keep cleaning simple. If it isn't a functional item, think twice before putting it there.

Keep everything used in the bathroom in the bathroom. Keep everything else out of the bathroom, including scuba gear, hamsters, and Nintendo games.

Use lemon-oil furniture polish to remove soap scum from glass shower doors. My friend Geri taught her family to use a squeegee on the doors after each shower. Your husband might not go for this, but the kids will enjoy it.

Keep a can of non-abrasive cleanser next to the tub and instruct family members to wash out their own rings after each bath. I learned the hard way not to use gritty cleanser after paying to re-glaze a bathtub. Now we use the foaming type of tub cleanser. Now I spray on the foaming bubbles type of cleanser, let it set a couple of minutes, then wipe away and rinse.

SUGGESTED BATHROOM RULES

Whoever uses the last of anything (soap, toothpaste, etc.) is responsible for writing it down on Mom's shopping list. No one can complain if Mom doesn't buy something that isn't written down.

Anyone leaving a mess in the bathroom gets to clean the whole bathroom. Your kids won't forget this rule after the first infraction.

Whoever uses the last arm's length of toilet paper must put up the new roll. This rule avoids having your kids leave just one square.

SUGGESTIONS FOR THE MASTER BEDROOM

Clean out and rearrange your closets and drawers. (See Classy Closets chapter.)

Wash the windows and air out the room. Vacuum and dust every corner. Wipe down walls and woodwork, lamps and knick-knacks.

Launder all sheets, blankets, and mattress pads. Flip and turn the mattress to prolong its life. Clean bed pillows according to manufacturer's directions. Replace old pillows--they get heavy due to filling up with dead skin cells which attract dust mites which, in turn, cause allergies and asthma. (Yuk!) To help protect against such creepy nastiness keep an allergy-free covering on your pillows. Make a list of any linens that need to be replaced.

If you don't have a ceiling fan, you can put a small, clip-on fan on your headboard. You can also purchase tiny, clip-on lights for late-night reading without disturbing your spouse. A slowly circulating fan makes the room feel fresher at night.

Explore new ways to make your bedroom a cozy, attractive private place for you and your husband. Put scented oil rings on the lamps. Install a dimmer switch on the lights. Put a CD player in the room with an assortment of mood music. Use your imagination!

Consider rearranging the furniture for a new look. After we installed new bedroom carpeting one year, my husband asked, *"Why don't we try putting the bed on a different wall?"* My first response was negative, but we tried it and he was right. That simple change made the room look twice as attractive as it did before.

Try making a tempting reading corner with a comfortable chair, a warm afghan and a lamp. Put a basket of magazines next to the chair.

Make a place for your husband to put his personal things when he changes clothes after work. He will be less likely to throw items on the bed or the floor if he has a convenient place to put them.

Be sure you have a lock on your door to insure privacy. Teach your children to knock when your door is closed—and do the same for them.

SUGGESTIONS FOR THE CHILDREN'S BEDROOMS

Wash all bedding and turn the mattress.

Arrange closet rods and shelves so that children can reach them to put away their own things.

Use inexpensive shelving and see-through plastic containers to organize toys, books, and puzzles.

If the room is too crowded to clean well, why not create a playroom in an unused room of the house or in the basement? If you can do this, put all toys in the playroom, leaving only stuffed animals and books in the bedroom.

Give each child his/her own clothes hamper and teach him how to use it daily.

Make sure school-aged children have a well-lit study desk or table with pencils, paper, etc. This encourages better study habits.

Post a calendar and personal household duties schedule for each child in his or her own room. Encourage self-reliance by teaching the child to refer to this often. Do *not* allow a television in your child's room—ever.

SPECIAL PROJECTS FOR FAMILY ROOMS

Consider creating use-oriented spaces. Make a quiet corner for table games or reading. Make an entertainment area around the CD player and television. Make a sewing or crafts corner.

Move furniture if traffic patterns are wearing paths in the carpeting.

If you don't use your formal living room except for baby showers and funerals, consider converting it to some other use. Make it the children's playroom or home school. Make it your personal office or craft room. Or let your husband put a pool table in it, as one woman I know did. It's too expensive to heat and air-condition an unused room.

SPECIAL PROJECTS FOR THE DINING ROOM

Remove everything from the china cabinet and clean it well. Wash or polish everything that you took out. Before putting everything back into the china cabinet, evaluate it. Do you ever use that silver cranberry dish? Do you really want to polish it again next year? Wouldn't it make a nice re-gift for your niece in Pittsburgh? Don't keep an item just because someone else gave it to you. It was probably once a white elephant in their china cabinet.

Evaluate your table linens. Do you have too many? Do you have enough? If you can sew a straight line, you can make matching tablecloths and napkins from fabrics or sheets. See if you have a tablecloth for your table with all the leaves in it, with only one leaf in it, and with no leaves. Make a notation of the size of tablecloth you need for each and keep it handy in your personal notebook or computer for future reference. You'll use that table more often if you have a tablecloth ready for each need, depending upon the number of your guests. Also make sure you have a table pad of tablecloth liner (I use a slightly smaller piece of cotton flannel) to put under the tablecloth to protect your table finish and provide a quieter surface.

See if you can use any of those rarely utilized serving pieces as decorations for your home. A platter with a letter opener on it makes a perfect place to put each day's mail. A bowl makes a good centerpiece when filled with flowers or sea shells. A pretty glass can hold cut flowers from the garden. Use what you have rather than letting it gather dust in a dark cabinet. With just a little thought, you can use many household objects as decorative items.

As you work, make a list of anything you would like to add to your dining room. Write it down in your personal notebook under *"Want List"* (see Chapter on Getting It Together) for the next time someone asks what you would like for Christmas or your birthday. Otherwise you'll never remember it, and you may receive another cranberry dish instead.

SPECIAL PROJECTS FOR THE KITCHEN

Clean out drawers, cabinets, and pantry. Wash them inside and out. If your shelving is too crowded, see what you can discard. How many pots and pans can you put on your stove at one time? How many plastic containers can one person use? Do you really want to wash and rearrange this item again next year? If not, get rid of it or donate it. Or have a garage sale.

Group similar items together for easy access. Put all glass bottles and jars on the same shelf. Organize all canned goods, all baking supplies, and all paper products on another. Have a section for the metal gadgets and another one for the plastic ones in your gadgets drawer. Then you have half as much to root through to find something.

Reorganize out your spices, throwing out any that are old. When you buy new spices, label their date of purchase with a piece of masking tape. A good place for storing spices is on little lazy Susan's in the small cabinet space that most kitchens have over the stove. Or put them in a drawer, name side up.

Clean the oven and oven racks.

Clean the refrigerator and freezer.

Reorganize your cookbooks and get rid of that pile of magazine recipes that you've been meaning to use for the past ten years.

Make sure you have a 6 to 12 month supply of food and water on hand in case the truckers strike or a natural disaster occurs. Have you ever noticed the panic at the grocery store over something as small as a forecasted snow storm? Keeping a decent supply of food on hand is a prudent precaution. If there ever is a panic at the grocery store you won't be part of the problem. See www.fema.gov for recommendations on emergency food and other emergency items. Take it seriously. How many natural and man-made disasters do we need to see on television to realize that the unthinkable can happen anywhere and anytime?

SPECIAL PROJECTS FOR THE BASEMENT

Clean walls, floors, and windows. Paint unfinished walls and floors with a light, water-sealing paint to discourage dampness and mold. Have your furnace and air-conditioner cleaned and serviced for safety and longer life. Buy a year's supply of furnace filters. Install a carbon monoxide detector.

One man told me how one winter he spotted some carbon monoxide detectors on sale as he walked past them at the hardware store, threw one in his cart, and placed it in his basement when he got home. Shortly thereafter the alarm went off and he thought, *"Oh, I got a defective one!"* He reset it, and again it sounded. Upon further investigation he realized that his basement actually did have deadly levels of carbon monoxide fumes! If he had not brought home that detector he would not have lived to tell this story.

Call the termite man and ask for a free inspection. They usually charge for inspections only if you're moving. When I was a nurse visiting inner-city patients I often came across many roach infested homes. I learned that little plastic *"Combat"* brand discs killed every roach with a few days, and were not a danger to people or pets. The roaches crawl in and then carry the poison back to their nests. And they are cheap! But they don't kill spiders. The number one way to eliminate spiders is a thorough cleaning and eliminating the dark, dusty, quiet hiding spots that draw them. Get everything off the floors and onto walls or shelving. Spray for insects or use natural repellents like borax, which my friend Jen says is great for deterring spiders.

Get rid of everything you don't need and don't want to clean and rearrange again next year. This includes dried-up paint cans, rusty bicycles, and Legos if your children are now in college. This can be a great time to make a few extra dollars by selling items you no longer need on Craigslist or eBay.

SPECIAL PROJECTS FOR THE GARAGE

Drag everything out of the garage. Sweep the floor, cleaning up grease and oil spots. Paint unfinished concrete with garage floor paint to make it much easier to keep clean.

Get rid of everything you don't need, and don't put it back there. Many home fires begin in the garage due to chemicals and trash stored there. I learned this after watching a friend's home burn nearly to the foundation. She and the children only barely made it out alive due to an alert jogger.

Get everything possible off the floor. Use one shelf for auto-care products, one shelf for garden chemicals, and one shelf for barbecue supplies. Put garden tools, shovels, etc. on the wall. Hardware stores now carry many neat organizers for garages.

If you have a garage window, make sure it's clean and the curtain is in good repair. The appearance of your garage from the outside is as important as the rest of your house. If you have a front-entry garage door, train the family to keep the garage door closed. Do you have a place where you could install a side access door? The inside of a garage is rarely a pretty sight for your neighbors.

My husband just installed a wonderful electronic garage door attachment that closes the doors at a set time after they have been left open.   Now we no longer worry about forgetting to close them when we leave the house. And more than once we have slept all night while the garage doors were wide open.   Even lightening had opened our automatic garage doors in the past. This is no longer a concern.

These are all just suggestions to help you get started on those deep-cleaning, reorganizing Special Projects. Use them all, or none at all. You'll surely think of many new ideas as you go along. Don't try to everything the first time around; just do what you can find the time for. You won't do it at all if you dread it, so make it as pleasant as possible. Just remember that your primary goal is to be happy with that room at the end of the month.

<u>ACTION ASSIGNMENTS</u>

- *Choose a weekly time for your Special Projects, whether it be one morning a week or during your weekly cleaning time.*
- *Make a monthly list of goals for your Special Projects.*
- *Itemize the things you plan to accomplish this month during your Special Projects time, and check them off as you accomplish them.*
- *Make a shopping list of what you will need and buy it before workday.*

4

GETTING IT TOGETHER

"Oh, for heaven's sake! Nothing is going right today," Margie complains for the tenth time. And, indeed, nothing is going right for Margie.

She is rooting through her drawers and cabinets for a measuring tape so she can figure out what size curtains she needs for her living room window. She's already upset because she bought curtains last week only to discover that she ordered the wrong size. Today she has to return them. At first she couldn't find her sales receipt, and now she can't find the tape measure. Little does Margie know that when she gets to the store to reorder the right sized curtains, she'll find that they don't come in the same shade of blue that she ordered the first time. Then she won't know which of the other shades of blue are right. Is this one too dark? Does that one have too much green in it?

Yes, Margie is having a bad day, and it's only going to get worse. The saddest thing about it is that Margie could have avoided all these hassles if only she knew the tips that you're going to learn from reading this chapter. After *"getting it together"* by making little organization areas in your home, you will never again suffer the needless frustrations that are overwhelming Margie today. You will have, as your mother always said, *"a place for everything, and everything in its place."* You may even have it a whole lot more *"together"* than your mother ever did. The whole purpose of this is not only to avoid needless

49

irritations, but also to save time. Every minute you save by being organized is another minute you can spend on doing things you like to do. That makes the time you invest in this chapter time well spent.

YOUR RECEIPT BOX

How many times have you thrown away or misplaced a receipt, only to regret it later? You tried on that pretty new sweater and it looked fine. How could you know that three weeks later the seams would start to unravel? You thought you had a great bargain on that pair of shoes until they developed a squeak with every step. Or you bought a dress for your niece's birthday only to learn that it was the wrong size and needed to be exchanged.

I'm sure you can think of dozens of instances when it would have saved you time and money if only you could find that elusive sales receipt. Many stores will give you a cash reimbursement for any sale item if you can prove that you paid full price for it in the past week or two. Some stores will allow you to return a purchase months later if you haven't used it and can prove you bought it there. But it's such a bother to keep those little slips of paper around, and you can never remember where you placed them even if you didn't throw them away. The only sane answer is to make yourself a receipt box.

You can make a receipt box out of an old cardboard shoe box or out of a pretty metal cookie tin. Mine is a small hinged plastic chest that I bought at a garage sale for ten cents. Just be sure to put the box in one spot and leave it there all the time. The best spot is probably in or near your desk.

Once you have your receipt box, you must adhere to only one rule: Save every receipt. Never throw one away. Never leave one in the shopping bag. Never fall prey to the temptation that *"I surely won't need this one,"* because that's the very one you will need. Just get in the habit of throwing every receipt in your receipt box as soon as you get home. If the receipt is not from a computerized register that automatically tells you what item you purchased just jot it down on the receipt.

Keeping these receipts helps immensely with your budgeting. We enter every receipt each week into our budgeting program on the computer. We put each purchase in the correct category. My husband loves this at tax time since everything he needs to do our taxes is already at his fingertips.

At the end of each month put all your receipts in an envelope and mark it with the month and year. At the end of the year, place all your monthly envelopes into one large manila envelope and date it with the year. Place it in your filing cabinet in the *"Taxes and Finances"* section. Your receipts can serve as valuable tax records. Best of all, your receipts can prove invaluable in budgeting for the next year. You'll know exactly where all the money went and which months had the heaviest expenses last year.

Your receipt box helps you save money now on any necessary returns or exchanges, and it also helps you to budget more wisely for future purchases. Best of all, it doesn't cost you a cent. Now that's what I call a bargain!

YOUR TOOLBOX

If you don't already have your own personal toolbox, I urge you to get one. No woman should have to root through her husband's stuff for any reason. First, you probably will waste time looking for whatever you need. Second, every time your husband can't find something, he will automatically assume that you were the one who misplaced it. It's wonderful to be able to say, *"I never go near your tools, honey. I've got my own."*

You don't have to rush out and buy a fancy red steel toolbox, although that can be an advantage if you want to put a lock on it. (This is not a bad idea—my husband and sons have already misplaced two whole sets of my tools.) You can simply make a toolbox out of a peck basket from the vegetable market, or out of a shoe box. I covered my peck basket with leftover wallpaper. You might want to glue lace and buttons on yours.

51

There's no rule that says a woman's tool box can't be pretty!

Here are some suggested items to put in your toolbox:

A small claw hammer

An assortment of regular and Phillips head screwdrivers

A box of small nails and screws

A measuring tape

A small pad and pencil

A packet of felt stick-on pads to protect tables from being scratched by figurines, etc.

White all-purpose glue

Put anything in your toolbox that you may need for the maintenance projects that you do around the house. Be sure to do what I've finally learned to do—mark your tools with colored tape or red fingernail polish so that you can identify them when they get borrowed by other people.

YOUR ERRAND BAG

Have you ever driven to the library and realized that you forgot to bring the books you wanted to return? Ever get to the cleaners only to find that you forgot to bring the dirty clothes? How many times have you walked into the grocery store without your shopping list and coupons?

These and many other frustrations can be eliminated by making yourself an errand bag. Mine is just a large plastic beach tote. You could just as easily use a large shopping sack or a box with handles. The important thing is to have an easily-carried container where you can place whatever needs to go on your next round of errands.

Keep your errand bag in the bottom of the coat closet or right next to the door so you don't forget it when you leave. In it place anything that needs to go somewhere else. A birthday present you need to take to a friend. The kid's video that needs to be returned to the library. Your husband's shoes that need to be repaired. The package that needs to go to the post office.

Your errand bag not only saves time by eliminating last-minute searches through the house, but it also saves the time, gasoline, and frustration spent on extra trips. An added bonus is that your errand bag eliminates the clutter of all those little *"orphans"* stranded in your house that have no place where they belong. Now they have an out-of-the-way place to stay until they leave. Best of all, your life is a little bit simpler.

YOUR DECORATING KIT

Even though you may have no intention of redecorating your home, it's wise to keep a decorating kit in your car. You never know when you might come across a terrific sale on tablecloths, the prettiest little pillow, or a gorgeous picture that might be just the thing for your bedroom. You just never know when you'll need to decide whether something will look right in a particular place in your home. And you never want to buy the wrong thing. How can you know if that item is the right shade of green, or if it will clash with the pattern in your wallpaper? I can't think of a better way than by having your own decorating kit on hand.

A decorating kit is simply a large folder or envelope filled with little pieces and snippets of things from your home. In it place paint chips or scraps of wallpaper from the rooms in your house. Put a little silk flower from the arrangement on your coffee table. Include a sample of your carpeting. (You can cut a sliver from the edge of a covered floor vent.) Save a snip of fabric from your reupholstered sofa. Add a piece of linoleum from the new kitchen floor. Fill your kit with anything and everything that you might ever need to help match or coordinate any future purchases you make for your home. It's even better if you throw in a few color snapshots of the rooms in your house.

In your decorating kit you can also place a small notebook filled with information about sizes of tables, windows, beds, or anything else that would help you get the right-sized item. Do you know what size tablecloth you need for your dining room or kitchen table? With one leaf, or two? When making up your decorating kit, take note of these things and you'll have the information forever.

Now keep that folder in your trunk or under a car seat and forget it—until the next time you just can't decide whether to buy the lavender candy dish or the blue one. The answer is as close as your decorating kit.

YOUR CHECK-OUT BOOK

Are you a book lover? Do you collect books? Do you love to lend those books to friends? Do you wish to ever have them back again? If so, you should make yourself a checkout book.

Use a small blank-page book or little spiral notebook to keep track of all those favorite books, magazines, and C.D.'s that you loan to friends. We all know that every friend intends to return those things soon, but too many of them get misplaced and forgotten. I've learned that the only way I remember who borrowed what is to keep track of it in my check-out book. There I write the name of the person, the item lent, and the date. Months later when I'm wondering where in the world my favorite cookbook has gone, I look in my check-out book and see that I lent it to Mary Lou. I simply give her a call and ask, *"Are you finished with that cookbook I lent you on April 17?"* *"Oh, did I forget to return that to you?"* she asks. *"I'll bring it over right away."*

Keep your check-out book and a pen right in your bookshelf. When someone borrows a book, write it down immediately or you'll forget. When they return the book, cross it off. Be sure to write your name and phone number in the front cover of all your books, too. It helps the borrower to remember where it came from so she can return it without being asked.

Don't wait too long before asking a friend to return a book. Once I asked for a book over a year after I lent it only to be told, *"I'm sure I gave that back to you a long time ago."* Three months is plenty of time for someone to borrow a book. If they haven't read it by then, they never will.

"Never a borrower or a lender be," unless you have a check-out book. Then your books will always return, like little lost sheep, wagging their bookmarks behind them.

YOUR FIRST AID CENTER

If your medications are cluttering and overflowing the medicine cabinet, drawers, and counter tops, you can quickly make a first aid center. Simply purchase several rectangular plastic baskets or small plastic chest of drawers that will fit into a high shelf in your bathroom linen closet and place a label on each one.

Mark one label *"Colds/Flu."* In that basket place all your over-the-counter and prescription remedies for treating flu, coughs, colds, and sniffles. This includes antihistamines, cough syrups, lozenges, and nasal sprays.

Mark another basket *"Stomach."* In that basket place any medications for stomach or intestinal upsets, such as antacids and laxatives.

Label another basket *"Pain."* This one is for any pain relievers such as aspirin, acetaminophens, ibuprofen tablets, ear drops, sore muscle rubs, and prescription pain relievers.

Then make a basket marked *"First Aid"* for adhesive bandages, gauze and tape, ace wraps, and medications for the skin. These can include aloe gel for burns, antibiotic gel, cortisone cream, suntan lotion, and anything else you may have for wounds or rashes.

In your last basket place your thermometer, ice bag, and heating pad. This is a good place to put booklets with first aid instructions. Be sure you have syrup of ipecac and instructions for how and when to treat poisoning, along with your local poison control phone number. Include a card with CPR (cardio-pulmonary resuscitation) instructions, and review them periodically. Sign up your family for a CPR and first aid class. Your teenagers will get more babysitting jobs if they let parents know that they've been trained in CPR and the Heimlich maneuver.

Where should you put your medication baskets? They must be in a safe location away from children—yours and other's. You never know when you'll have an unexpected, or even uninvited, visitor. We once had a little neighbor boy who was an expert at sneaking into houses unannounced and consuming anything in sight, including my neighbor's birth control pills and my make-up! The best place I can think of for keeping your medications center is on the top shelf of your linen closet. Be sure to install a flip lock on the door.

Once a year, while doing your *"spring cleaning,"* be sure to go through all your first aid supplies and throw out any expired medications. Make a list of anything you need to restock. Then you'll be comfortable knowing that you are prepared for any emergency.

YOUR CLEANING CENTER

Let me send you on an impromptu scavenger hunt. Can you quickly find the following items?

Dustpan and brush
Bucket and sponge
Dust cloths & cleaning rags
Floor wax or cleaner
Silver and brass polishes
New vacuum sweeper bags
Squeegee and window cleaning solution

Time's up—did you find them all? Were they located in one convenient place or did you have to do a lot of searching? Did you find the bucket in the garage, the silver polish in the back of the china cabinet, and all the other cleaning supplies scattered in cabinets and drawers throughout the house?

If you had any trouble locating these items, the simple solution is to make yourself a cleaning center. Your cleaning center is one specific place where you store all your cleaning tools and chemicals. The purpose for having it is to save time and effort—and to avoid scavenger hunts. It can be located wherever you want to put it.

One good spot for establishing your cleaning center is in a laundry room closet, if you're fortunate enough to have one. If not, how about making a special place in a corner of the garage, or in the pantry, or some unused closet in the house? If none of those places are available to you, there is another possibility—the linen closet. Almost every house or apartment has a linen closet. Most linen closets just become cluttered repositories of old sheets and pillowcases plus an odd assortment of other equally unused items.

If you have a washer and dryer at home, how many sets of sheets do you really need for each bed? My guess is only two—one set on the bed, which you wash and put right back on each week, and an old set for a spare. Keeping more than two sets of sheets per bed is an extravagance if you don't have space for a cleaning center. Donate your extra sheets—and anything else you don't use—to charity or put them in a garage sale. Then store your one extra set of sheets plus any extra blankets in a drawer, a chest, on the top shelf of your closet, or in under bed cardboard storage boxes. Or you can lay them flat between the mattresses. Towels and washcloths should be kept in the bathroom. Now you have space in which to make your cleaning center!

To convert the linen closet to a cleaning center, simply remove all but the top two or three shelves, leaving enough room below them to accommodate your vacuum cleaner and broom. Install hooks around the sides and back wall for hanging your sweeper attachments, mops, and brooms. Save the top shelf for your first aid center if needed. Use the other shelves for storing your cans and bottles of cleaning chemicals. If there is room next to your vacuum sweeper, purchase a small utility cart with shelves for storing items such as your clean rags, sweeper bags, sponges, squeegee, etc. Otherwise store them in a bag hung on a wall hook. If room permits, you may also want to have a basket for storing light bulbs and a small one for storing unused extra batteries. (Can you ever find them when you need them?) This is also the perfect place for storing your toolbox.

As a very important safety precaution, install a lock on the door of your cleaning center to prevent accidental poisoning of a child. Even if your kids are grown, you'll feel better when guests bring children over to visit if you know that your cleaning chemicals are behind a locked door. You can purchase simple, cheap *"flip-locks"* at the hardware store. They easily install at the top of a door on the hinge side, and all you do to lock the door is close it and flip the little lock with your fingers. Now you know everything is safe.

YOUR FAMILY MESSAGE CENTER

The most likely place for your family message center is probably in your kitchen—everyone shows up there sooner or later during the day. Install a bulletin board with a pad and pencil near the telephone. Post a family activities calendar with plenty of room to write down everyone's appointments. Have the children write in their after school activities and sports practices. Enter important dates from their school calendar onto the family calendar as well.

Be sure to place a pad and pencil next to every telephone in the house to insure that messages will be taken. If your family members have to walk to the kitchen to write it down, they may get distracted.

The family message center is also the place to put inter-family memos such as *"I need the car Friday night"* or *"Can someone drive me to Francie's house Sunday at 2:00 p.m.?"*

It is very important to instruct all family members in the correct manner of answering the telephone. *"Smith residence, Sandy speaking. No, she isn't available. May I take a message?"* Then instruct them to always write down the message—otherwise it will be forgotten—and put the note on the bulletin board.

Note: Don't allow very young children to answer the telephone. Have you ever tried to get a talkative toddler off the line? *"Can you please call your mother to the phone, Sweetie?"* This can be very annoying to the caller, but worse yet, it can be a dangerous situation for a child not mature enough to understand how to handle calls from malicious strangers.

THE BABYSITTER BOOK

Purchase a spiral notebook to use exclusively for your babysitter's information. On the inside cover make a list of all important phone numbers: the poison control center, ambulance, police, fire department, pediatrician, and nearby relatives or next-door neighbors.

Below that make a checklist of things to show a new babysitter. Go over that list with her the first time she comes to your home, and remind her each time. Show her where you keep your first aid center, where telephones are located, how to operate the door, locks, and light switches in your home, etc.

Then use the lined pages in your notebook to write specific instructions for each babysitter visit, which you can tear out after coming home. Write the phone number where you can be reached, the time you expect to be home, and who you prefer her to call if she can't reach you. Write down what snacks you allow the children to have, what TV shows they may watch, and what time the sitter should get them into bed. If they're taking medication, write down instructions for that as well. Note anything she needs to know such as, *"The baby won't go to sleep unless she has her pink blanket and teddy bear."* Your children and your sitter will appreciate the information. And you won't be worrying about them while you're supposed to be having a nice time away from home.

KEYS, PLEASE!

I hate to ask such an embarrassing question, but have you ever locked yourself out of the car? Wasn't it traumatic—and inconvenient? Didn't it make you feel foolish? These are very good reasons for making some extra sets of keys and putting them in some important places.

First, make sure that every family member old enough to use them has a house key and a set of car keys. Then make sure you have an extra set of each in a hidden place inside your house just in case someone loses a set. (Mine hang on a nail inside the coat closet.) Make an extra set of keys to give to a trusted neighbor if they are needed in an emergency, such as when you are out of town.

Then get an extra house key to keep in a hidden place outside your house in case you or the children are locked out. (Your trusted neighbor won't always be home.) Just wrap the key in a plastic bag and find a good spot that a burglar wouldn't consider. (No, not under the doormat or flowerpot.) How about behind a loose brick, under a particular rock, or under the back deck? Put your heads together, come up with the best spot, and make sure everyone knows where it is. If someone uses the key, be sure it gets replaced.

Finally, get two extra sets of car keys for each car. Keep one set in your purse. Most women don't lock their keys and their purse inside the car at the same time. Keep the second set hidden in a magnetic holder somewhere on the outside of your car. I believe that getting locked out of the car—especially at night—is a greater risk than having a thief find the car key and steal the car. Besides, a car thief doesn't usually waste time looking for a key; he just breaks in.

This may seem like a lot of extra key making, but this small investment will avoid the trauma and inconvenience of having a family member locked out of the house or car, especially in the cold or at night.

Shortly after I hid an extra set of keys on the outside of the family car, my husband locked his keys in the car when we went to church. He didn't realize his mistake until after the service. Being a basically ornery person, I let him stew for a minute before telling him where to find the extra key. But when he found that key, I got one big kiss. Talk about a lot of satisfaction for just a little effort!

These are a few sure-fire, family-tested suggestions for organizing your home and your life. Once done, you will be a happier, more organized, and *"together"* homemaker.

ACTION ASSIGNMENTS

- *Work on implementing all systems that you wish to use, but do them one at a time, completing one before beginning the next one.*
- *Before beginning each project, make a shopping list of any items needed and have everything on hand.*
- *Include the family by explaining the benefits of the new system and instructing them in its use.*
- *Have a family conference to review the way telephone calls are to be answered in your home. Let each child practice. Explain that from now on there will be a no shouting policy in your house. Install a room to room speaker system if needed.*

5

YOUR CONTROL CENTER

If you've ever watched a space rocket launch on TV you've seen the control center from which all the activity of the event is conducted. Men sit behind rows of desks monitoring, directing, and correcting to make sure all goes according to plan. What's the result of their effort? Everyone claps and cheers as a shining missile pierces the sky and disappears into outer space.

As the manager of a busy home and active family, you need a control center, too. You need a place where you can formulate and execute goals and projects for yourself and for your family. You need a central place in your home from which all production emanates. You need a control center so that you, too, can achieve your goals—keeping your home from careening out of control.

Your control center is, of course, your office. Whether it's a whole room or just a little nook in the corner of a room, your office is the place where you correspond, pay bills, plan, and organize. If you've never had an office of your own, this chapter can help to transform your life. If you already have one, this chapter can help you make it even better.

FINDING A PLACE

The first step toward making an effective office is to decide upon its location in your home. When I

63

decided that we needed an office and I couldn't find a place for one, I decided to do something drastic. I took over our seldom-ever-used formal living room to convert it into an office. You should have seen the look on my husband's face the day he noticed there wasn't a stick of furniture in our previously furnished living room!

"Where is our furniture?" he gasped, wide-eyed.

"I sold it," I smiled with all the feminine charm I could muster.

"You what?" he cried incredulously.

"We never used it anyway, and I'm going to make the living room into a place that really gets used," I said, trying to sound convincing. I gave him a reassuring pat and said, *"Trust me."* (Sometimes it's better to ask forgiveness than permission!)

My husband was even more shocked the day he found a large, old, battered desk sitting in the middle of the empty room—and me scooping goopy furniture stripper from it.

"Don't worry, honey. It's gonna look great!" I smiled.

By this time I guess he figured I was a hopeless case. But we got many years of use from that formerly idle living room. My desk, which I rescued from the back of a used furniture warehouse and spent hours refinishing, was used daily.

Today my control center is located in a new home with a small office that looks out of two front windows. I can work for hours, emailing friends, blogging or running my online business, while watching neighbors walk by and the cats sitting on the windowsill just inside a row of cheery rose bushes. I am surrounded by tall bookshelves filled with favorite books, family photos and memorabilia. I really enjoy working there because I love the ambience there.

Maybe you don't have anything resembling a good spot for an office, and you can't imagine where to find space for one.

You may need to make your temporary office in a spare dresser drawer or in an under bed cardboard box, and hope for more space of your own in the future. Better to have a tiny office than no office at all. Don't despise the day of small beginnings. It's okay to start out with just a laptop and a few folders.

But chances are you, too, could find an under-utilized spot in your home—a living room, dining room, sitting area, or just a corner in the bedroom or kitchen. If so, begin to make it into a functional office and get some real use out of that space. Think creatively and you'll probably find a great place for that new *"control center"* of your own.

FURNISHING YOUR OFFICE

Once you've decided on a location, you need a desk. Perhaps you already have a desk in an obscure area of your home, doing little more than gathering dust. If so, it's time you think about using it more productively. Perhaps you have a built-in desk in your kitchen that you haven't utilized until now because it didn't seem large enough. If you need to purchase a desk, you don't need to run to the nearest furniture store to pay retail prices. You could rummage through some garage sales and find a used desk that just needs a little sprucing up. Or you could visit some re-sale shops like I did. If you let it be known that you need a desk, you might find a relative or friend who has one she no longer wants. You can also make a desk by laying a door or piece of painted MDF (ask the hardware store to cut it for you) over two file cabinets—it creates a large work space and lots of storage space, too. Even a plastic-top utility table from your big-box discount store can serve the purpose until you find a desk that's just right for you.

Along with your desk you'll need a chair. I used a dining room chair until I got a great rolling office chair for $10.00 at a garage sale. If you have a spare wooden chair, you could attach casters to the legs and make it into a rolling desk chair. Just make sure it's a comfortable height for you or it can cause backaches. Your office chair needs to be high enough that your elbows rest comfortably on your desktop without raising your shoulders or causing you to hunch over.

Then you need some neat stuff to put in that desk of yours. Along with all your favorite photos and desktop memorabilia, you need some serious desk supplies. You need a lamp that will not glare in your eyes. If it is a nice wooden desk you need a desk pad to protect it from scratches and ink marks.

If you aren't sure what kind of computer you need consult your husband, friends, or the local computer store. You may choose to use a portable laptop instead of a stationary computer. Or you may be satisfied to have a multi-use cell phone with internet functions or an iPad if you really don't need a complete computer set-up.

Then you need *"In and Out"* trays—these are crucial. You can buy expensive teakwood or woven basket trays, the inexpensive plastic stacking trays work just as well. Get four. The top tray is for *"To Do"* material that you have not yet processed. The second tray is for *"Bills To Be Paid."* The third tray is to *"Hold"* for follow-up later. And the fourth tray is *"To Be Filed."* These trays will do wonders for your paper management!

After you bring in the mail from the mailbox, don't lay it in your *"To Do"* tray. Find another place to put each day's mail until you and your family have sorted through it. You can purchase a mail holder designed just for that purpose, or you can use a pretty basket, tray or dish. Place the mail holder wherever it's most convenient, perhaps on your desk or on an end table or the kitchen counter. Keep a letter opener and a wastebasket near your mail holder.

After looking through your daily mail, all the discards go right into the trash. Any reading material, like magazines or catalogs, can be placed on your night table or in a basket next to the sofa for idle evening browsing. The only thing that goes into the *"To Do"* desk tray are papers that need further processing at desk work time. That leaves the *"To Do"* tray free from the clutter of junk mail, unwanted envelopes, or reading material.

Here are other supplies you may want to acquire for your office:
- Calendar

- Pens, pencils, markers
- Scissors
- Transparent tape
- Stapler and staple remover
- Paper clips (colored ones are more fun!)
- Rubber bands
- Ruler
- Envelopes
- Cards and stationery
- Stick-on *"Post-It"* notepads, various sizes
- Calculator
- Your receipt box and monthly envelopes
- A large wastebasket (your greatest ally in the war against paper clutter!)

I keep my greeting cards in a separate box that has dividers marked for the type of card (birthday, thank you, plain, etc.). This allows plenty of room for storage and protects them from damage. Shop at the cheap card store once a year to re-stock, or make your own creations.

Have you ever wondered what to do with personal cards and letters that you receive? Do you regretfully throw them away, or do you stuff them into any available spot and worry about what to do with them later? If so, you may want to start storing them in a jumbo sized zip-lock bag in your desk drawer. Write the year on the outside of the bag. At the end of the year you can store it in your memorabilia box. I keep a large cardboard box for each member of the family stored in the basement. That's where I store treasures that we don't want to throw away, such as special artwork, letters and cards, etc.

Some women like to take all the year's memorabilia and make it into scrapbook pages, or even collages. See how creative you can be!

YOUR FILING SYSTEM

The next most indispensable item that belongs in your office is a file cabinet. No, you don't have to be a business office to need a file cabinet, you just need to be a busy family. Without my file cabinet I would never be able to find anything. It saves a lot of squabbles, too. No more irritated voices saying, *"I didn't lose it—you were the last one who had it! How am I supposed to keep track of every little piece of paper?"* Now that we have a functional filing system, I often wonder how we ever found anything before using the *"stuff it wherever you can find an empty spot"* system.

If you don't have a file cabinet, you don't necessarily need to buy an expensive metal drawer-style cabinet. Department stores and office supply centers now carry great sturdy cardboard *"banker's boxes"* made for that purpose for only a few dollars, which are great for long-term storage, too. There are beautiful plastic or woven file folder holders of all shapes and sizes that look attractive stored on bookshelves.

Before we get into the specifics of how to set up your filing system, it's important to keep one thing in mind. According to one estimate, eighty percent of papers filed are never looked at again! To avoid creating an ever-growing filing-system monster, it's imperative that you set aside a time each year to go through every piece of paper in your filing system. Thin out your file by discarding unneeded papers, and re-organize anything that got misfiled. If you have the computer space you may choose to scan in important documents rather than store the paper. The best time to do this is early in the year, before tax time. It could be your Special Project for the month of January to clean the office, desk, and files.

You'll also need to purchase a box of file folders. Then gather all your family papers and sort them into logical divisions. Rather than having a random assortment of alphabetically arranged file folders, divide them into major categories and sub-categories. For instance, the first major category hanging divider in our file cabinet is marked *"Automobiles."* Behind that are file folders for each of the sub-categories: a folder for *"AAA."* auto club information, then a separate folder for each car. Inside each of the folders for our cars we keep every piece of paper relevant to that car, including receipts from state inspections and repairs and maintenance, including oil changes. (I know a woman who used her records to win a court case against a car dealer who refused to honor her warranty. He said he didn't have to replace defective parts on her car because she hadn't changed the oil on schedule. But she had written proof that she did!)

Set up another major category for *"Family Information"* with folders for each family member's medical and dental insurance records, children's report cards, birth certificates, and other such personal papers. Behind *"Household Information"* you could have folders for keeping those dozens of little brochures and warranties that come with every appliance and gadget you own. Inside each brochure staple the warranty and a photocopy of your receipt, which also shows the date you purchased the item and its cost. You can also make a folder for keeping a copy of all information about your house, including a survey of your lot.

Make a major category for *"Finances"* where you keep folders regarding investments, loans, etc. In a folder marked *"Credit Cards"* keep photocopies of all credit cards and information on where to call if they are lost or stolen. Make a folder for *"Taxes"* where you throw any relevant information throughout the year, including W-2 forms, pay stubs, donation receipts, etc., to make tax time a lot easier. Maybe you want a folder for *"Misc. Financial Info."* where you can keep magazine and newspaper clippings about budgeting and investments. Keep a copy of your will in a folder marked *"Will,"* and let family members know where it is if they ever need it. Give a copy to anyone who needs it if something should unexpectedly happen to you. Be sure to keep any irreplaceable important papers, such as original copies of your will, deeds, and car titles, in a safe deposit box. Make photocopies for your home filing system. Make a videotape or take photos of everything in your home to keep in your safe deposit box for insurance purposes.

It's nice to have one file drawer or box for important household information. Use another drawer to store your interests and hobbies. Under the major category of *"Vacations"* keep folders for each trip you've taken in the past so you can remember where you stayed and what you saw. Keep copies of maps, motel receipts, and sight-seeing brochures. It makes planning the next trip a lot easier. Collect brochures for planning new trips in another folder.

I keep a large category marked *"Personal Interests."* Behind that I have folders labeled with such unremarkable things as *"Amish"* (I love to collect articles and photos about the Amish), *"Decorating,"* *"Favorite Anecdotes"* (I love funny stories), *"Gardening,"* *"Gift Records"* (where I keep track of gifts I gave in the past to avoid duplication), *"China and Silverware Patterns"* and dozens more.

If you have a lot of information on one subject, you can make that a major category. If you enjoy collecting recipes, you could have the major category of *"Recipes"* with subcategory folders marked *"Beef,"* *"Casseroles,"* *"Chicken,"* *"Desserts,"* *"Fish,"* etc. Then if that major category becomes too large, just give it a whole file drawer of its own. My *"Quilting"* file grew until it had to go into a separate filing box, which I now keep with my sewing supplies rather than in my office. Other major categories you might want to create could include *"Bible Studies,"* *"Crafts,"* or *"Children's Interests."*

Do you collect stacks of magazines that you can't bear to part with because you don't want to lose many of the photos and articles they contain? Has your stack become so large that you couldn't find something in there if you had to? Are you tempted to throw out the whole thing? Your filing system is a great place to resolve that problem. As you read your magazine, earmark the pages with information that you want to save. Then tear out just those pages and throw away the rest. Then just drop those clippings (or photocopies of information from books) into the appropriate folder in your system, and you can retrieve them anytime you need them. With this system you never waste an idea—once you store it in your files, it's yours forever. When we remodeled our kitchen I was glad to have many photos of kitchens in my

"Decorating" folder to give me ideas. Whenever I get in the mood to crochet, I just pull out the folder that's stuffed with great patterns I've collected over the years.

When reading magazines I also tear out any cartoons or articles that I think a friend or family member might enjoy. I lay them in the *"To Do"* tray on my desk until I sit down to write letters and enclose the clipping in the envelope. My sons at college often received such little reminders that I was thinking of them.

What do you do with catalogs and magazines that you no longer want? There are many ways to recycle such paper products other than sending them to the recycling center. Why not take them to a nearby hospital or leave them in the dentist's office the next time you visit?

GIFTY BAGS

One of my favorite things to do is to make little *"gifty bags"* for friends and nearby relatives. Whenever I have something I'd like to pass on to one of them, I just put their name on a paper sack or a pretty plastic bag (I save the nice ones for this purpose) and toss in the bag anything I come across that I think they would like. When you meet your mother at the mall gave her a gifty bag that contains a catalog that she likes, a couple of family photos, or the recipe for a dessert you recently enjoyed.

The last time I saw my friend Janice I gave her a goodie bag that had a CD of a Bible teacher we both enjoy, a cartoon clipping, a bookmark, and a magazine. Right now I have a gifty bag waiting for the next time I see Susan. It contains several magazines, a hand-me-down T-shirt for her son, and a snapshot both of us sitting at my sewing machine the day she came over and we made vests together.

This is a great habit to begin among friends—soon they'll get the idea and start giving goodie bags to you, too! It's a resourceful way to have something to give away at little or no expense. Keep your little gifty bags in your large errand bag so you'll have them with you the next time you're on the go.

As you can see, there are many creative ways to tame the paper tiger at your house. Your new control center not only helps you organize your papers—it helps you organize you. Your new office (no matter how small) is where you can do your daily planning and have your quiet time, as well as shuffle papers. It's important to have one regular day per week when you take the time to do desk work. Perhaps one evening a week after you put the children to bed would be best for you. I enjoy doing my desk work on idle Sunday afternoons. Find the day that best suits you, and mark it on your weekly schedule.

To keep your desk supplies from *"walking off,"* it's wise to show your desk to your young children (they're going to be curious!) and explain to them that they can't remove anything from your desk unless they receive permission from you. Then they'll probably want you to help them set up a desk of their own—which is the best idea yet!

ACTION ASSIGNMENTS

- *Select a location for your new control center.*
- *Equip your control center with a desk and a comfortable chair.*
- *Make a shopping list and obtain any needed desk supplies.*
- *Set up your new "In and Out" trays and filing system.*
- *Find a permanent place to lay each day's mail until family members sort through it.*
- *Keep reading material on a bedside table or in a large basket for later perusal.*
- *Begin to make "gifty bags" for friends.*
- *Show your children your new control center and explain the rule about not removing items from your desk.*
- *Help your children set up a desk of their own where they can study and keep their own papers and supplies in order.*

6

CLASSY CLOSETS

"Honey, the boss just asked me to take an important client and his wife out to dinner tonight, and I'd like you to go with me. Can you be ready in an hour and a half?"

When Ellen answered the telephone that was the last thing she expected to hear. She stood there wondering how she would make the transformation from her present condition—she had been cleaning the house—to that of charming executive's wife, in only ninety minutes. She knew this was important to her husband, and she didn't want to disappoint him. Their daughter was spending the night with a friend, so at least she wouldn't have to worry about finding a sitter.

"Well, I guess I can make it," Ellen replied before hanging up the phone. Then she jumped into the shower, blow-dried and fixed her hair, and put on her make-up in only forty-five minutes. *"Great!"* she said, *"I've still got another forty-five minutes to get dressed, so I'll be ready in plenty of time."*

That's when her troubles began. Ellen threw open her closet door only to face a confusing jumble of clothing and accessories. What on earth should she wear?

First she pulled out a navy blue knit dress, put it on, and looked in the mirror. *"Rats! I forgot about those deodorant stains under the arms. I meant to take this to the cleaners after I wore it the last time."*

She pulled that off, messing her hair in the process, and tried on a black and white printed skirt and blouse. *"Oh, no,"* Ellen sighed as she realized there were two buttons missing on the front of the blouse. She threw them on the floor next to the navy blue dress.

Next she donned a red and green plaid dress with a pleated skirt. When she tried to zip it up, Ellen remembered that she was about eight pounds lighter the last time she wore this dress. *"Darn it!"* she mumbled in exasperation as she rooted through her closet for something else.

Forty-five minutes and several unsuccessful outfits later, Ellen dashed out the door wearing that navy blue dress. *"I'll just have to keep my arms down,"* she reminded herself. She was also wearing scuffed navy pumps and pantyhose with fingernail polish patching one end of a runner that she hoped wouldn't grow any bigger. She hadn't had time to put on a touch-up coat of nail polish, or to carefully select the proper jewelry and scarf.

Did Ellen have a good time at dinner? Of course not. Why? Because Ellen didn't feel good about herself that night. And Ellen didn't feel good about herself simply because her closet was a mess. If only she had taken a day to clean and organize her closet, Ellen would have enjoyed the beautiful restaurant, the delicious food, and the people she was dining with. But the only thing she could think about all evening was herself. Ellen learned a valuable lesson that night—*one must think of herself ahead of time so that she can think of others later*. The very next day Ellen organized her closet.

MAKE THE INVESTMENT

A woman is not going to look any better than her closet does. The woman with the messy, disorganized closet is going to have that messy, disorganized look. But the woman who makes you look twice because she has that self-confident, classy appearance also has that secret ingredient—a classy closet.

Classy closets don't just happen, though. Like everything else worthwhile, they take an initial investment of time and effort. So before jumping headlong into that deep, dark closet, take a few minutes to do some advanced planning.

First, set aside a day for that closet make-over. As a wise homemaker, you'll want to tackle this project on a day when you have a minimal amount of distractions. Send the children off to Grandma's for the day, or arrange for them to play at a friend's house. You may even want to strike a bargain with a neighbor. *"If you keep the kids while I clean my closet, I'll return the favor for you."*

Before you embark on that special *"closet experience,"* make a shopping list. Take a look at what you have versus what you need, and buy your supplies in advance. You can, of course, pick up the phone and have someone come out and re-build your closet from scratch. If money is no object for you, this is a great way to do it. But for the rest of us who are accustomed to do-it-yourself projects, I suggest you consider purchasing whatever you need from the following list of closet spruce-up supplies:

- Light colored paint if walls and woodwork are dingy.
- Specialty closet rods and shelving for making more space. A double rod is essential in at least part of your closet for hanging skirts, blouses, and slacks.
- Good storage containers for out of season clothing. Don't allow last season's clothing to waste valuable space.
- Three large boxes to use on closet cleaning day. Label them: *"To Dry Clean," "To Repair or Alter,"* and *"To Charity or Garage Sale."*
- A container or basket to keep in your closet. This is where you throw anything that needs to go to the dry cleaners or to be repaired. If you leave it on a hanger, you'll inevitably forget about it.
- Plenty of padded and wood hangers. Good clip skirt hangers. Don't bother with gimmicky hangers where you hang several things on top of each other. You'll tire of bothering with them. Plan on recycling all those old wire and plastic hangers.

- Shoe racks. Get the simple metal floor-type or, if you have the wall space, the pocket-type is nice. Get only as many as fit in your closet comfortably. Limit the number of your shoes to what fits on these racks.
- A good quality belt hanger. Plastic ones usually break. The ring-type is a pain because you have to take off all the belts in front of the one you want, and then put all the others back. I have found a men's peg style necktie rack to be the perfect belt hanger.
- Scarf hangers. Storing scarves in drawers always leaves them creased and crushed. At a luggage shop I found some clip clothespin-type hangers for hanging washables when traveling. They allow clipped scarves to hang freely from the closet rod instead of lying folded. Or you may want to drape them on a mug rack.
- A full-length quality sheet glass mirror. You just can't be well-dressed without being able to see your whole self at once.
- A frilly sachet to give your closet a fresh, clean scent and make it as pleasurable for your nose as for your eyes.
- A good lint remover and a hook to hang it on.
- Hooks for hanging hats and accessories on unused wall-space.
- Organizers for storing purses and folded sweaters. Never put sweaters on hangers or they'll pull out of shape.
- A large dirty clothes hamper. One with wheels is nice for rolling to the laundry room.
- A shoe shine kit supplied with polish and clean rags. You can always tell how well-groomed a person is by looking at his or her shoes.
- A small pair of scissors for clipping tags and loose threads. Have you ever succumbed to the temptation to pull that little thread, and wished you hadn't? Hang the scissors on a hook.
- A small wastebasket for throwing out threads and tags.
- Anything else you can think of that will make your closet, and therefore your life, a little nicer.

- Keep in mind that you can always return what you don't use, so buy plenty ahead of time.

Once you've acquired your supplies and set aside a day all to yourself, you're ready to dig in and clean your way out. Before you start, be sure to make your bed and straighten your room. You want a cheerful atmosphere to work in, don't you? Put on your favorite closet-cleaning music, perhaps something inspiring and classical, like Vivaldi's *"Four Seasons."* Open a window and let the breeze freshen your room as you work. Pull back the curtains and let the sunlight pour in. After all, today is the day that you and your closet are making a fresh beginning. You may as well make it fun!

GETTING STARTED

The first step is always the hardest, so just get it over with. Yes—Take Everything In There Out of There! Yes, *everything!* The clothes. The shoes. The belts, scarves, sweaters, jackets, and all that weird stuff that you wonder how it ever got there in the first place. Pull it all out and throw it on the bed. When you finish, you should be staring at one naked closet. Shocking, isn't it? But don't worry, you are not just applying a band aid here; this is major surgery!

Next, replace that burned-out light bulb and shine up the fixture. Now you can see to wash down the walls and wood-work, shelves, and clothes rods. If you decided to freshen up the paint, see how quickly you can get that done. Turn up the music and go at it with enthusiasm. *"Whatever you do, do your work heartily, as for the Lord"* (Colossians 3:23). Finish up by washing or vacuuming the floor, and you'll have a pristine, clean closet looking back at you.

You have just completed Phase I: Emptying and Cleaning. It's time to fix a cup of tea, clear a spot on the bed, and relax a minute while admiring what you have accomplished. You haven't just emptied a closet—you have prepared a clean slate. From now on you are going to be *very* selective about what goes back in there. No more junk! Nothing even questionable.

Nothing that doesn't fit perfectly, isn't pristinely cleaned, pressed and repaired. Nothing that doesn't look fabulous on you, Darling! Only classy clothes are going to be allowed into your classy closet.

If you share your closet with your husband, I suggest you replace his clothing fast. (If he comes home before you finish, you don't want him to think you're moving him out!) As you probably know, living compatibly with your husband is much easier if each of you has your own closet. But if you must share, just choose a side for yourself and make the most of it. However, you might be able to think of a place where you can have a closet of your own. One woman I know moved her clothing into a spare bedroom. My husband and I shared a tiny walk-in closet until I discovered an alternative. I transformed a little-used sitting nook in our bedroom into a second closet. That new closet was a lot more functional than that useless nook ever was.

TRY ON EVERYTHING

Now you are ready for Phase II: Trying On and Sorting Out. Take time to try on each garment in front of your full-length mirror. Carefully scrutinize each item. Before determining where that garment belongs, ask yourself the following questions:
1. Is it out of season? If so, be sure you clean and repair it before putting it in storage. Anything out of season is wasting your precious space.
2. Does it fit well? If the answer is no, it goes into the alteration box or the give-away box—not in your closet. If you have to lose *"a couple of pounds"* before it fits properly, store it with your out of season clothing. You don't want to look into your closet and see anything hanging there that you can't wear *today.* This is your personal boutique, not a storage locker.
3. Is it comfortable? If it isn't, you won't wear it. Get rid of it. It will surely be comfortable on someone else who could really get some use out of it.
4. Does it need cleaning repair, or alteration? Put those items in the box so labeled.

5. Is this a flattering color for me? If you aren't sure, hold it under your face in good lighting. Does it make your face look pretty and bright, or does it make you look older and sallow? If it isn't a color that's good for you, you'll never feel good about yourself when you wear it. Let it go to someone who would look better in it. By letting go of things you make room for new ones.

6. Can I mix and match this with other clothing? Try on new and different combinations to see how far you can make that item go. Different prints and stripes can be attractively mixed if they are in the same colors but differing scales. Completely different solid colors can be mixed if they are of the same intensity. You may find a new use for a neglected item.

7. Have I worn this in the past year? If you haven't, why not? Perhaps your closet was so overcrowded that you forgot you had it. Or maybe you didn't realize it looked good with some other clothing you have. Or did it just need the hem shortened? If so, keep it. But if you didn't wear it because it's poorly constructed, doesn't look right on you, or you're just plain sick of it, get rid of it. I find that if I'm really tired of something I never get over it.

8. Is this something I dislike, but just feel too guilty to throw out? If so, do it anyway. *You won't save any money by letting it hang uselessly in your closet.* Consider whatever you paid for it to be the price of experience. In the future you'll shop smarter. Besides, if it's given away it really isn't a waste. If donated, you can even make it a tax deduction.

9. Is it modest? While some may insist that, *"Cleavage is in,"* to those of us who seek to please Jesus rather than the world, *"Modest beauty is in!"* And tempting men's eyes to look at your exposed breasts is definitely *"Out!"* The way we dress is a daily testing grounds for where our hearts really lie, in The World or in The Kingdom of God. Low necklines and high hems are never in good taste where it really counts. And wearing too-tight clothes to try to look thinner or sexier on makes us look like a walking stuffed sausage!

Try an experiment. Spend the entire day wearing a lovely modest blouse and a long below-knee length skirt and sweet flat shoes, and see if you don't feel a whole lot more beautiful and graceful than you did in those short-shorts, that tight t-shirt and flip-flops. Ask God to tell you which was more beautiful to Him. Which appeals more to you, the look of Desperation or the look of Moderation? Do you prefer to attract stares, or respect?

Now that you have decided which garments are worthy of your classy closet, and neatly hang each one on an appropriate hanger. Put jackets on padded hangers, skirts on clip hangers, and fold slacks neatly on slacks hangers. Return all those nasty metal hangers to the dry cleaners for recycling. While you're at it, throw out all plastic dry cleaning bags and paper sacks—they are definitely not classy. You'll wear everything in your closet often, and you won't need to store anything in bags or plastic.

Hang all your garments facing the same direction. Group blouses, slacks, etc., neatly together. See that all buttons are buttoned and zippers zipped. Of course, everything should be impeccably clean and pressed. Polish your shoes and purses and set them pertly in their proper places. Put belts and scarves where they belong. From now on, everything that goes into your closet is truly *"ready to wear"* in its best condition.

From now on, whenever you open that closet door you'll feel as pampered as if you had your very own boutique where everything was designed especially for you. Your most private, personal space has become your favorite place! Every time you emerge from that closet, you're going to look as great as it does.

After seeing your closet transformed, you may very well want to tackle those dresser drawers, too. Why stop halfway? Group similar items together in the same drawer, and throw out all bags and boxes. Keep jewelry neatly organized in a jewelry box, not scattered randomly in several drawers. If it won't all fit in your jewelry box, maybe it's time to give some of it away or sell it on eBay. Get rid of all your *"holely"* underwear and that ratty nightgown that turns off your husband.

He surely won't mind when you get new ones. Make that dresser as neat and clean and classy as your clothes closet.

Attack your make-up stash in the bathroom. Do you really need 37 different shades of eye shadow? Or all those dried-up vials of fingernail polish? I know you have that shoebox full of samples and cosmetic rejects, too. Did you know that old make-up breeds bacteria? If you don't wear it, trash it. From now on set a limit to the space you'll allow for cosmetics, and don't fall prey to temptation in the drug store anymore. Just remind yourself of all those messy, drippy jars and bottles that you just threw out.

YOUR WANT LIST

Now return to that closet for another good look at what you've accomplished. Once you've tried on every garment you own and determined its fate, you may be surprised at how bare your closet looks. *"Good grief—I have a huge pile of cleaning, repairing, and giveaways, but very little in my closet!"* you gasp. But that's good! It has been estimated that *most women wear ten percent of their clothing ninety percent of the time.* You've just weeded out some of those things that you never wore anyway to make room for the things that you really do enjoy and wear. Besides, your garments need space to breathe. *"But this is too much breathing space!"* you protest.

That's when you go into Phase III: Planning Future Acquisitions. Once you've disposed of your giveaways and returned clean, repaired clothes to your closet, you're ready to make a list of needs and wants. Keep this list in your personal planner or phone notes so you'll have it with you at all times. Sit down in front of your closet and thoughtfully plan what items you need to round out your wardrobe. Write the most important items at the top of your list.

Maybe you need a versatile, neutral-colored dress that you can dress up or down, depending on your accessories. Because you can get a lot of mileage out of this one piece of clothing, you should invest in quality merchandise. Perhaps you need a couple of fun blouses in bold colors to brighten a too-conservative repertoire. Write down anything and everything you would like to incorporate into that new classy closet of yours.

Then you must make a promise to yourself: in the future you must never buy anything—clothing, shoes, purse, or accessories—without first looking at your *"want list."* Seeing something that you really want will prevent you from making an impulse purchase of a *"bargain"* sale item. *Remember, it isn't a bargain if you don't need it!* And if it isn't on your list, you don't need it.

Your list will be invaluable the next time someone asks you what you would like to have for your birthday or Christmas. Never again will you stare blankly and say, *"Oh, I really don't need anything."* Instead, you'll say, *"Well, there's a smashing pink and green silk scarf at my favorite dress shop!"* Why not allow them the pleasure of giving you something you'll really use?

The main advantage of your list, however, is to help you avoid future mistakes in your closet. It encourages you to purchase only those things you need. Don't try to overcome your insecurity about how to dress well by over-buying. Don't try to substitute quantity for quality. It is much better to have a limited selection of quality clothing than to have a closet crammed full of misfits, *"bargains"*, impulse buys and make-dos.

You may want to study books that will help you avoid future clothing mistakes by determining the look that is right for your body size and shape. Too often we try to look like someone we are not for the sake of wearing what is now *"popular."* Why not just be yourself? Everyone else is taken! If you are a full-time homemaker, why not look like a lovely homemaker instead of trying to look like a bank president or a rock star?

Confusion about who we really are often causes us to follow every new fashion trend, regardless of what looks best on us. It takes courage to proudly define ourselves to the world. I once read that fashion says, *"Me too,"* while style says, *"Only me."* Learn what style is really You based on your body proportion and lifestyle, and upon your own strong sense of self-value. Once you've found the right style and coloring for you, every piece of clothing you purchase will mix and match with a lot of other items in your closet. As a result you'll need less, so you can buy better quality, and wear it with unapologetic confidence. All the right *"things"* worn by a woman who doesn't know her true worth to God only falls flat. It is that deep down knowledge that, *"I am loved by the only One whose opinion really matters,"* that gives us that glow. Walk tall, imaging that your head is connected by a string to heaven, and no one will imagine that you ever doubted yourself!

STRETCH YOUR BUDGET

Sometimes we feel too guilty to pay more for the quality we really want. The best way to determine whether a garment is worth the price is to calculate the cost per wearing. Divide the cost of the garment by the number of wearings to see what kind of buy you're getting. For example, a faddish dress that costs $60.00 and is worn only four times actually costs you $15.00 per wearing. But a well-made, classic styled dress that costs you $200.00 and you wear twice a month for the next couple of years costs you little more than $4.00 per wearing. So the *"costlier"* item was really the better buy.

Perhaps that's why the excellent wife in Proverbs 31 wore *"fine linen and purple."* That was as well-dressed as you could get in those days. But, far from being extravagant, she also did her own sewing. This is something that still works today for the woman who wants to dress well on a budget. I'm not a great seamstress, but I don't mind making a basic, simple skirt because I enjoy stretching my clothing budget. My friend Barb is an excellent seamstress who makes almost all the clothing for herself and for her children. She has developed her talent through taking sewing and tailoring classes, which are available to most of us who are willing to learn. She loves to economize while making things exactly the way she wants them.

Another way to economize is to purchase clothing that mixes and matches so that you need fewer items. I have a magazine article that shows how you can combine eight garments thirty different ways! Making each garment go a long way helps us resist the impulse to over-buy clothes. But clothes aren't the only thing we can over-purchase.

Eunice was a woman who owned hundreds of pairs of shoes. If anyone commented that her collection rivaled that of Imelda Marcos, Eunice would laugh and reply, *"Well, at least I bought them all on sale."* As a result, she had disorderly closets stacked full of shoes that she rarely wore. She couldn't even remember what shoes she owned, let alone wear them all regularly. Then an awful thing happened—her foot grew a size! (This happens occasionally to the best of us as we age.) No longer do any of those hundreds of pairs of shoes fit her.

Like most women, I have a weakness for pretty shoes. But years ago I decided I didn't want to become a shoe-aholic, spending limited clothing funds on compulsive shoe-gratification. I wanted to have a neat closet. I wanted to know how many shoes I owned, and I wanted to wear them all, rather than letting them grow cobwebs in the dark recesses of my closet. So I purchased two shoe racks and allowed myself only as many shoes as I could fit on those two racks. If I bought a new pair, another pair had to go.

As a result, I rarely buy a new pair of shoes today. But when I do, I look for shoes that are very versatile in colors that can be worn with a lot of things in my closet, rather than glitzy, faddish styles. I also find that having fewer pairs of shoes makes it easier for me to keep them polished and in good condition, making them last longer. Since I don't buy a lot of shoes, I'm not forced to shop for a bargain every time. I hate paying full price for anything, but if I must do so to get just the right thing, at least I'm sure to get my money's worth.

This attitude about shoes has become my attitude about my entire wardrobe. I'm a great believer that, with wise purchasing, less is more. As women who desire to be faithful stewards of our finances and attractive representatives of Christ, we must continually exercise wisdom in achieving balance between too much and too little. And it is a constant challenge.

The closet-organizing business is booming in America today because we're trying to stuff too many unnecessary things into our closets and into our homes. I've seen the tiny closets that our grandparents' generation had, and it makes me ashamed of my greed.

Shopping has become a dangerous national pastime, tempting us to want much more than we need. We are then tempted to leave our homes for careers to finance our credit cards. Our families become consumer-oriented rather than home-centered. Meanwhile, we spend a fortune to *"dress for success,"* all the while yearning for the good old days when we were homemakers who were content to wear jeans and a t-shirt. It's one thing to go to work because we've made a deliberate decision to do so, but quite another to find ourselves stuck in a job we really didn't want just to pay for things we really didn't need.

So, go ahead and make that *"want list,"* but don't let it rule your life. Good things come to those who wait, as they say. As a result of your sensible planning, when those things do come, you know they will be right for you. And you'll take care of them and make them last.

Meanwhile, you can enjoy the freedom that comes from simplicity. No longer are you bogged down with stressful clutter. All your clothes look great on you, and you know that they are ready to go when you are. Best of all, you look like a very classy lady, because you have one *really* classy closet!

ACTION ASSIGNMENTS

- *Select a day that you can spend cleaning out your closet. Write it on the calendar. Arrange for babysitting if needed.*
- *Make a shopping list and purchase needed supplies before your "closet experience."*
- *On the appointed day, clean out your closet using Phase I: emptying and cleaning; Phase II: trying on and sorting out; and Phase III: planning future acquisitions.*
- *Make a "want list" of items you need to round out your wardrobe. Plan wisely, then stick to your plan. Keep that list in your personal planner.*
- *Decide to get dressed to please Jesus each morning, rather than the world. Teach your children to do the same.*

7

ARE OUR HOURS OURS?

"Time is the coin of your life. It is the only coin you have, and only you can determine how it will be spent. Be careful lest you let other people spend it for you." (Carl Sandburg)

Effective time management is the art of taking charge of how you spend your life, minute by minute, hour by hour. We are all given the same amount of time each week. But what we accomplish with those 168 hours varies widely from person to person. Each of us has different things we want to, need to, and have to accomplish with our time. Wise time management, which is crucial to achieving these goals, makes the difference between the achiever and the person who just muddles unhappily through life. If YOU don't plan how you will spend each day, be aware that the world, the flesh and the devil will be happy to do it for you! The world will intrude with its *"urgent and important"* (*not!*) requests, your flesh will tell you that you need to flip on that TV and munch down a sack of potato chips while watching a soap opera, or the devil will tell you to take off for the mall and rack up a few hundred dollars on your charge account. *So be wise and plan ahead, and then stick to your plan.*

The best time management tool in the world is learning to say *"No."* Do not say yes to anything that you do not want to do, do not have time to do, or you are unsure of. It is always the wrong thing to do. If

89

you are not yet assertive enough to smile and say that little word unflinchingly, I suggest that you practice saying this sentence out loud until it comes out easily: *"Let me think about it. I'll get back to you."* Then get up your nerve to say *"No"* later, when you are prepared. Learn to say it with no excuses or apologies--that is important. Giving excuses just allows the other person to try to *"fix"* it for you, making you have to give another excuse, then another. Just say, *"I thought it over, and I'm going to have to say no to your request. I'll let you know when I have more time to help out."* End of conversation. I estimate that this habit alone can save the average homemaker twenty-seven years of busy-work in her lifetime.

Another great time saver is to abstain from the following bad habits: watching meaningless television shows, reading junk literature (like most novels), spending aimless hours on the telephone, and cleaning things that aren't dirty.

One formidable time waster is the habit of living from crisis to crisis. People who are controlled by the tyranny of the urgent are usually people who do not plan. In fact, crises are caused by lack of planning! Plans prevent the expected from becoming the urgent. Having a personal datebook will do wonders toward correcting that problem.

YOUR DATEBOOK

The most important step to take in managing your time is to manage yourself. The first step you can take to manage yourself is to have a datebook with which you plan your days. Keep this datebook in your purse when you leave the house. This means it needs to be small enough to fit into your purse easily. The only time it needs to be out of your purse is when you're home. Then you'll want to refer to it often. If you have a datebook that's tailored to your own personal needs and you use it daily, it will liberate you from the tyranny of time pressure.

Many people now use their Blackberries or iPhones or similar devices for keep track of their calendars. I still prefer my old fashioned paper type of calendar. Just like books, I prefer having something I can feel, hold and write in with a real pen. Stores carry dozens of different datebooks to help manage the busy lives of the career woman. I've found most of these daily planners to be useless to the career homemaker. You don't need to keep track of customers, business expenses, or mileage. You don't need to know what time it is in Japan or Europe. You do need to know which child needs to be carpooled at what time, when it's your turn to bake cookies for the Girl Scouts, and the size of your furnace filter when you're standing in front of them at the store. I personally use a <u>Day by Day</u> planner that I order every December from <u>www.Datebook.com</u>. It's just the right size for me after I tear out all the pages I don't use in the front and back of the book. I use the monthly calendar so I can see the entire month when scheduling my activities. This helps keep me from loading too many activities into one week. Find whatever really works for you.

Develop the habit of looking at this calendar every morning before you jump into your day, and you won't forget another task or appointment. Better yet, you won't schedule yourself to be in three different places at one time. And if someone asks, *"Can you babysit my pet Chimpanzee next Tuesday?"* you simply whip out your calendar (which is always with you for such moments) and reply, *"Sorry, I have another appointment that day."* (You do not need to reveal that your appointment is with your dog in the park.) It gives you a great sense of power to discover that no one argues with a woman who has a datebook!

Keep a large, lined Post-It inside your calendar to jot down your *"To Do"* list. Any time you think of something that needs to be done just jot it down there. The best way to decide which item should be done first is to ask yourself, *"Which one of these things will I be most happy to know tomorrow that I did today?"* Then complete each item in order of importance before going on to the next. If you get only one item done each day at least it will have been the most important one. Each morning review your list, scratching off those tasks you accomplished. Your daily *"To Do"* list eliminates worry, confusion, and guilt.

Also keep a personal *"Want List"* inside your calendar or daily journal. Right now my list includes *"new 60 x 90 drapes for guest room"*, *"flower arrangement for coffee table"*, and *"house slippers."* This list also comes in handy whenever my husband asks, *"What would you like for your birthday?"* I used to go blank and say, *"Oh, I don't know."* (Can you ever think of something good when you are asked?) Now I whip out my *"want list"* and say, *"Well, there's a nice sweater that I've had my eye on."* Why not use your want list to help someone else with his gift list?

And somewhere in the back of your datebook should be a miscellaneous list where you keep certain information that just doesn't fit anywhere else. This is the perfect place to write down the size of your furnace filters, for example. List the sizes you need for tablecloths, with and without table leaves. What kind of ink does your printer use? Have you ever forgotten the model number when you get to the store? I'm sure you can think of similar things that would be helpful to you.

You may also want to keep a running gift list of things you need to buy throughout the year. When you come across a nice sale you can review who has a birthday coming up, what size they wear, etc. Gift information is always handy, especially since birthdays and Christmas have a habit of coming every single year.

As you can see, a personal datebook, whether on paper or in cyberspace, is a lifesaver for the woman who is serious about managing her time and enjoying her life more fully. Whether you use my suggestions or design it according to your own personal needs, the important thing is that you have it and use it!

CULTIVATING A QUIET TIME

Having a daily, morning *"quiet time"* with God is essential for the woman who wishes to have a calm, directed day. I have practiced the discipline of a daily quiet time for decades now. I can assure you that it's one of the most important personal disciplines you can practice. The days that I've rushed into action without pausing for those precious minutes of prayer and solitude have convinced me of their importance—I am invariably distraught and/or disorganized before the day is over. That's why I don't often forget to take those few early morning moments for myself.

I suggest that your quiet time be early in the morning, rather than later in the day or in the evening. King David repeatedly referred to his morning prayers, saying, *"In the morning, O Lord, Thou wilt hear my voice; in the morning I will order my prayer to Thee and eagerly watch."* (Psalm 5:3) It only makes sense that we offer God, the Giver and Sustainer of life, the first fruits of our day.

It's also best to get into the Word before you get into the world. Once you get busy in your worldly affairs, time has a way of slipping by. How much better it is to cover yourself, your family, and your daily affairs with prayer for God's protection and guidance before springing into action. I've found this such an indispensable help that when I was working the 7:00 a.m. shift as a nurse, I set my alarm clock for 4:45 a.m. just to be sure I had time for my quiet time before going to work. Our work as homemakers is no less needy of God's provision.

How long should your quiet time be? That varies from person to person, of course. Why not start out with fifteen to thirty minutes? Just beware of the temptation of letting time get away from you to the extent that it interferes with accomplishing your daily tasks. I've known more than one woman who used her quiet time as an escape from more pressing duties. Under the pretext of being pious, they were actually lazy and self-indulgent. You can fool yourself, and maybe fool others, but you can't fool God. If you are not getting your basic chores done during the day, don't spend more than a few minutes on your daily *"quiet time."*

The benefits of such a discipline are not only those that can be immediately seen or felt, although there are those. The major benefit of having a daily quiet time is a cumulative one. After many days, weeks, and months of sitting at the Master's feet, listening to His voice, and meditating on His Word, you are changed. You will take on a deeper peace, wisdom, and confidence. You can't help becoming more like Jesus after giving Him the prime moments of your day, day after day. You'll find yourself communing more with Him throughout the day, having established a close relationship each morning. After a while you find yourself speaking to Him whenever a problem or a decision arises. You ask Him to help you shop wisely as you enter the grocery store. In short, you begin to practice the presence of Christ in your moment to moment life. This alone is worth taking the time to sit at His feet when you are tempted to hurry on to other things. You find that you don't need to spend as much time in reciting prayers when your life actually *becomes* a prayer.▯

Whenever I have my quiet time, there are always three books at my side. The first, of course, is my Bible. The second is my datebook, with all my day's plans written in it. I can pray over my schedule as I have my quiet time. If anything else I need to do comes to my mind (some people call them distractions), I just quickly jot it down in my datebook and proceed with my prayers. Perhaps I remember that I should phone someone, or drop a card to a sick friend on my prayer list. Perhaps I remember that I need to schedule an appointment to get the car fixed. By the time I finish my quiet time, my day is planned!

The third book that I have with me during my daily journal. Mine has always been nothing more than a 3-ring loose-leaf notebook. This is because I never know how many pages I'll need to fill in a year, so I can always add more. I have tried pretty published journals from time to time, but I never had enough pages to make it last through a whole year. Here I write my thoughts to God every day. Some days it's just meaningless drivel to anyone other than me, like what I did yesterday, or what kind of weather we're having. Other days my journal contains heart-wrenching prayers or psalms of praise. It's quite a potpourri of thoughts that I've written over the past many years, and it's rather fun to reflect upon occasionally. One important note on keeping a journal is to be sure your family knows to keep out; it is strictly your personal book. Be careful not to write any specifics that could be hurtful to someone else if it were read by another.

If you aren't much on writing, perhaps you want to just record the highlights of your life, or occasional insights into Scripture, opportunities you've had to minister to someone, or an encouraging word that God whispers to you in prayer. What godly aspirations has He deposited in your heart? Do you remember the last direction God gave you? Write it down! Your journal will help you to become more diligent in fulfilling God's will for your life. Your journal is for writing your prayers. Write them specifically. How else will you know when God answers your prayers unless you remember what you prayed? You will have a permanent record of events to thank God for. Your recorded prayers will remind you of God's faithfulness.

MANAGING YOUR MINUTES

Most of the time that we waste is not in large blocks but rather in small fragments. Like sand, productive minutes can slip, unused, through our fingertips. To avoid this, we must redeem those little nonproductive moments that meander through our day. We often waste our small moments because we think they're useless. But every sixty-second interval is just as useful as another, whether it is joined with others to form a large block or not.

We also waste our minutes because we think it takes longer to complete most tasks than it really does. That's why we concentrated on watching the clock while doing housework in *"Never Clean for Company"*. Most women are surprised to discover that it only takes three minutes to make a bed, and that they can do all of their housework much more quickly than they thought. One woman in my homemaker's class said, *"I can't believe how much time I've wasted all my life because I believed it took so long to do housework. The first time I concentrated on just cleaning the house while watching the clock, I learned that I could clean*

95

my entire two-story house in just two and a half hours. I had never done that before!"

If being aware of time can help us accomplish big jobs, it certainly can help us to accomplish a multitude of little jobs as well. The following list of small tasks can be completed in those short, idle moments we spend on such things as waiting for the microwave to finish heating, talking on the telephone, or waiting for the dog to come back inside.

- Clean a kitchen drawer
- Empty the dishwasher
- Scour the sink
- Sew on a button (keep a mending basket next to your favorite chair)
- Wash fresh vegetables
- Say a prayer
- Clip coupons
- Fix a lunch
- Sort through the mail

To make good use of those idle moments away from home, always take something with you when you leave the house. You can balance your checkbook while waiting at the doctor's office, work on a quilt while sitting through Little League practice, or read a chapter on money management while your daughter has her braces adjusted. If you forget to take something to do, you can use those spare moments to pray for your family, your friends, or for strangers around you. That is certainly productive. Let not a moment escape your grasp that you don't use intentionally, whether to accomplish something or to relax tired muscles and breathe deeply. The secret is to be fully conscious of your minutes. That's what life on earth is made of. Don't let it slip away!

ACTION ASSIGNMENTS

- *Practice responding to demands on your time by saying out loud, "I'll think about it—let me get back to you."*
- *Make a datebook.*
- *Begin a daily quiet time, even if it is only fifteen minutes.*
- *Make a quiet time journal.*
- *Practice being consciously aware of the value of each minute.*

8

GRACIOUS GIFT GIVING

The doorbell rings unexpectedly. When you open it you're surprised to see your friend Frieda standing there looking a bit distraught.

"Come on in, Frieda," you say, holding the door open.

"Oh, I can't stay, honey, I'm so busy. Just wanted to drop off this present for you," she gushes as she shoves a crumpled paper sack at you. "I know your birthday was a month ago, but I forgot all about it. Sorry I didn't have time to wrap it or get a card, but it's the thought that counts, right? I hope it fits—I had to guess at your size." As she heads back toward her car she calls out, "I've got to rush, darling. Let's do lunch soon, shall we? Happy birthday!"

You close the door and look forlornly at the paper sack in your hands. A peek inside reveals a beautiful sweater. True, it's not your size. True, it doesn't look a bit like you. But Frieda obviously spent a mint on this sweater. So why aren't you feeling too excited about this gift? And why aren't you feeling too excited about Frieda's friendship, either?

Then you remember how differently you felt when Susan gave you a birthday gift. It was just a little gift, a pretty sachet for your bureau drawer. But you felt so special the way Susan treated you that day. She invited you over for lunch on her back porch. You enjoyed a pleasant visit together, sipping lemonade and nibbling finger sandwiches. Then she gave you that little package all tied up in colored paper and fussy ribbons, with a touching card that she had made herself. Now whenever you see that little sachet in your drawer or smell its sweet scent, you remember a happy afternoon spent with a devoted friend.

No, it wasn't the gift that pointed out the difference between these two friends—it was the manner in which the gift was given. Truly, the way a gift is given says much more than the gift itself. And it says a whole lot more about the gift giver.

A gift thoughtlessly given—no matter how expensive—says loud and clear, *"This is all I cared to do for you."* But a gift given graciously says, *"You are so special that I took the time and effort to tell you so."* Isn't that the whole purpose of gift giving—to make a person feel special? When we give out of obligation or habit, rather than thoughtfulness, the effect is just the opposite.

Of course, all of us have been caught short at one time or another when it comes to gracious gift giving. But has unplanned gift giving become a habit, or is it an exception to our usual thoughtfulness? We don't want to fall into the pattern of the people who always act like birthdays and Christmas have caught them totally by surprise—as if they had no idea that these things always happen on the same day every year.

It isn't out of intentional thoughtlessness or carelessness that we become guilty of such things. It is simply because of over-busy, under-organized lives. The cure is to take a few hours and concentrate on correcting these problems ahead of time. Knowing that every effort invested now in planning and organizing our gift giving will pay off in many smiles when those gifts are given, let us begin. To become a gracious gift giver, you need to take the following five steps.

1. Make a gift budget.
2. Make a gift notebook.
3. Shop in advance.
4. Give creative rather than expensive gifts.
5. Make a gift center.

Let's look at each one in more detail.

MAKE A GIFT BUDGET

You and your husband need to decide together exactly how much you wish to allot to your annual gift fund. Then determine how you want to slice that pie. Do not be influenced by what other people spend. This is no time to think you are obligated to spend on someone else an amount comparable to what you think they spent on you in the past. They may, in fact, be very happy to see you tone down the spending on your end. Decide how much you will spend on your entire gift budget for the year, and then divide it up into birthday gifts, Christmas gifts, and other gifts like unexpected wedding or baby gifts. Don't forget to include the expense of purchasing gift supplies such as gift cards, wrapping paper, ribbons, and postage--they really add up. Put your gift budget in writing, and then write the monetary limit behind each entry on your list. Then stick to that budget. A budget won't benefit you if you don't use it faithfully.

Write the name of the recipient, the occasion, and the date for every gift you plan to give over the next year. Include friends, relatives, and anyone else you give gifts to each year. Be sure to make allowance for a couple of unexpected gift giving occasions, such as weddings, graduations, or new babies. Are you shocked at the length of your list? Review your list and see if there are any changes you should make. Are there any gifts that you're giving perfunctorily? Is it just a tradition that you send Aunt Fran a box of candy every year, and she sends you one in return? How about just exchanging cards instead? Or, better yet, a phone call? If you have a large family, could you suggest name-drawing at Christmas, or setting a price limit on each gift? Could you agree to limit gift exchanging to the children and let the adults exchange hugs and cookies?

Try to eliminate all gift giving that is done out of obligation alone. The Bible tells us that we are to give *"not grudgingly or under compulsion; for God loves a cheerful giver."* (II Corinthians 9:7) God also wants us to be wise stewards of our resources. Pray over each entry, asking for discernment and wisdom.

Once you have tightened up your gift list, you may want to consider adding some new names. Are there any people that you appreciate for their special kindnesses throughout the year? A kind mailman? A favorite checker at the grocery store? Have you noticed an elderly shut-in who never seems to have a visitor? You can brighten someone's life with a small, unexpected token of your appreciation or friendship at any time of the year. Perhaps your family would like to make a gift box during the holidays for a needy family. Our church encourages people to cut back on needless Christmas gifts and giving, instead, to a project that digs wells in undeveloped countries where death is attributed to lack of fresh water more than any other factor. Once you've eliminated the time and expense of frivolous gift giving you can plan these special acts of kindness that truly change lives and change the world.

MAKE A GIFT NOTEBOOK

This can be a small notebook, or it can be a separate section of your datebook. Today there are many nice gift apps created for your electronic devices, as well. Choose whatever works for you. However, creating your own can be done quickly and easily, without much expense. Your gift notebook consists of three sections. Make the first section a yearly perpetual calendar where you write the dates of every occasion for which you need to give a gift or send a card. This section always stays the same, except for occasional corrections or additions.

In the second section of your notebook, have a separate page for each person on your gift list. Put the person's name on the top of the page. Below that write the dates of when you give gifts or cards to that person, such as their birthday or Christmas. Behind each occasion write the amount of money that you budgeted for that person on that occasion. Below that write down all pertinent gift-giving information such as clothing sizes, favorite colors, decor of rooms in the home, special interests, etc. Use the space below that to jot down any gift-giving ideas that you may think of during the year. If you don't write it down immediately, you probably won't remember that idea when you go shopping. All this information goes on the front of each sheet of paper.

On the backside of these pages, write the following headings: *"Date," "Occasion," "Item,"* and *"Price."* Every time you purchase a gift, fill in the information in the appropriate column below these headings. This will serve as a permanent record of gifts that you have given each person, as well as a record of your gift expenses. Be sure to save every receipt in your receipt box. It will help you keep your budget on target, as well as coming in handy for any needed returns.

The third section of your gift notebook is a current yearly gift needs list. At the beginning of each year, starting with January, list in chronological order each gift and card that you need to give this year. So you may have *"January 6, Mom and Dad's anniversary. Send Card."* Your next entry may be *"February 21. Tom's birthday. Gift and card,"* and so forth throughout the year. Leave a space behind each entry to check off when you have purchased the card or gift. You'll have an instant, up-to-date record of what you need and what you have already obtained. If you include your Christmas gifts on this list, you can be doing your Christmas shopping all year.

Keep your gift notebook in your purse because you never know when you'll need it. The next time you come across a great sale, you can flip open your notebook, see exactly what your gift needs are, and take advantage of the sale. You won't get stuck wondering, *"Did I get Jane a birthday gift yet?"*, or, *"What size blouse does Grandma wear?"* Everything you need to know is at your fingertips.

SHOP IN ADVANCE

How many of us have allowed last minute shopping to take all the fun out of Christmas? And how many of us have an excuse for that, knowing that Christmas is coming again every single year, barring the Lord's return? The same is true of birthdays, anniversaries, and most other gift-giving occasions. So why wait until the pressure is on to shop? Last-minute shopping leads to poor gift selection, gross over-spending, and minor nervous breakdowns. Ever notice how the closer it gets to Christmas, the more sour the expressions on the faces of shoppers? They are obviously not enjoying the spirit of Christmas.

At a seminar I once attended, Gary Smalley, instructor and author, stated that one of the major differences between most men and women is in their shopping habits. Men, he said, are natural *"hunters,"* while women are into *"experiences."* When most men shop they are subconsciously seeking to fulfill that urge to *"hunt"* their prey, sack it, and quickly drag it home. Women, on the other hand, usually prefer shopping to be a pleasant *"experience"*-- perhaps an all-afternoon event that includes enjoying sights, sounds, smells, conversations, and even lunch with a friend. (This explains why most husbands and wives are not compatible shoppers!)

But whatever kind of shopper you are, last-minute shopping can turn you into a grouchy, desperate *"hunter,"* unable to experience any of the satisfactions that a pleasant shopping trip can bring. The major advantage of shopping in advance is that it is more economical, allowing you to compare wisely and to take advantage of sales. Whenever I'm tempted to buy something at full price a little voice in my head says, *"Everything is on sale sometime."* So why not purchase items that are marked down, rather than marked up? How often have you rushed out to buy a gift and found just the right thing on sale? Never? It seems that the greater the pressure to buy, the higher the price. Shop early and beat the system. Shop online and save the pressures of travel and crowds, if you please, but that means shopping in advance to allow time for delivery. You'll enjoy the process when you don't have time pressure, and you'll have the extra benefit having time to comparison shop for bargains.

GIVE CREATIVE GIFTS

Emerson said, *"Rings and jewels are not gifts but apologies for gifts. The only true gift is a portion of thyself."* A creative gift is a portion of yourself. It need not be expensive, only unique—contoured to the unique person being gifted. Anyone can walk into a store with a credit card and do a year's worth of shopping at one time. But a creative gift says, *"I went to the trouble to think of something special for you."* It beats the heck out of unimaginative gift cards.

A creative gift might be a snapshot of you and your friend at the zoo. It could be a mugful of assorted teabags. (Try browsing through the thousands of unique mugs available on eBay.) It might be something that only you knew the person would like to have. So why give the usual fare? Why not give your sports-loving brother a ticket to the baseball game packaged inside a new baseball cap? Take your niece, who is learning to play the violin, to an orchestra performance. Try a free outdoor concert followed up by a trip to the ice cream shop. Deep clean the inside of your husband's car. Teach a friend how to knit. Or babysit for a neighbor so she can do her Christmas shopping. Some of these gifts can be presented as a handmade *"coupon"* inside a birthday card.

Give a group gift instead of individual gifts. One year I gave my brother's family a group gift of a large popcorn container filled with a gift card for DVD movies, some individual microwave popcorn packages, and some movie-time candy. It was much for fun, and less expensive, than buying individual gifts for everyone. Another year I gave them a one year family membership to the Botanical Gardens. Think about experiences or food rather than *"stuff."*

A creative gift can also be a handmade gift. Receiving a token of your invested time and talent makes a person feel very special. One of the fringe benefits of being a full-time homemaker is that we can take the time to develop our create talents and then use that talent as a gift to others. Handmade gifts are the greatest fun to give. Some that I have given in the past are ceramic geese and Christmas ornaments, crocheted caps and scarves, knitted golf club covers, home-sewn tablecloths and matching placemats, greeting cards with envelopes made from my own photography, and home-baked cookies served on an attractive garage-sale dish.

If you *"don't know how to make a thing,"* don't despair—you can learn! Most communities have craft classes in adult evening schools. Sewing centers offer sewing classes for a nominal fee. You'll flatter relatives by asking, *"Could you teach me how to do that?"* (I learned to crochet from Great-Aunt Minnie.) One year I learned how to make pretty ladies' collars out of vintage doilies at a women's church group. I also took quilting classes at a local quilt shop and made many quilts as gifts over the years--money well spent. You can find endless craft ideas in the books at your library and online. Go to online for countless videos on how to sew, crochet, knit, or an array of other things. The opportunities for learning are overwhelming once you start looking. Never pass up an opportunity to learn a new skill. It is something you can use and something you can teach to your children. I'm so glad I learned what I am now teaching to my own grandchildren. They think I'm really smart!

Make your gift giving projects a family affair by including your children in the process. You will be teaching them the value of giving while teaching them skills. And you will be creating family memories while creating gifts. Take photos while you work to save the memories. Send a photo with the gift.

Encourage your children to make greeting cards. Our sons became quite talented at making personalized cards for any occasion. Now that they are grown young men, I like to get out the memorabilia box and look at the sweet and funny cards they made over the years-- what a laugh! Many of our relatives have their own similar collections of Scot and Todd creations tucked away where store-bought cards would have been long ago forgotten. Creative gifts are a blessing to the recipient and to the giver as well.

MAKE A GIFT CENTER

A gift center is a place where you keep all your gift wrapping supplies in one convenient spot. It can be as simple as a plastic under-bed storage box or as elaborate as a big walk-in closet (for those fortunate enough to have a spare one handy.) My gift center once consisted of an old card table next to a set of shelves in the basement. Today I have the luxury of an empty guest bedroom closet with sliding doors. I use the bed for wrapping boxes, and the closet for storing my supplies and gifts. I bought an inexpensive plastic stack of drawers at the local big box store. I use the drawers for ribbons, bows, gift tags, gift wrap, and gift boxes. I store large boxes and bags on shelving and in wire baskets. Get creative, use what you have or buy what you need. But make that special place and you will be surprised how much it improves your life.

I love my gift center because I never have to go scrounging through the house to find gift wrap, tape, or scissors.

To make your own gift center you will need the following supplies:
- Gift wrap (Save the Sunday comics for wrapping children's gifts.)
- Tissue for lining boxes
- Boxes
- Cellophane tape
- Ribbons and bows
- Scissors
- Ink pen
- Greeting cards
- Mailing boxes and shipping tape (Order free Priority Mail boxes from www.usps.com.)
- Waste basket

When you have made a nice present or have shopped in advance with the help of your gift notebook, you will actually look forward to wrapping it in your gift center. Attach a pretty bow and card and set it on the shelf, ready to go. Then when that occasion comes you will feel confident and gracious. Best of all, the person you are *"gifting"* will, indeed, feel special. Remember, it's not important how much you give but rather how much love you put in the giving.

<u>ACTION ASSIGNMENTS</u>

- *Make a yearly gift budget.*
- *Make a gift notebook or download an App onto your electronic device.*
- *Make a gift center.*
- *Think of some creative gifts that you can give.*
- *Take a class to learn a new craft.*

9

CURB APPEAL

Real estate agents use the term *"curb appeal"* to say that the outside of a house is attractive. If they drive their clients up to the curb in front of a house and the clients can't wait to go inside, they say it has curb appeal. Sometimes their clients take one look and say, *"Yuk! We don't want to see that—drive on!"* That house obviously lacks curb appeal.

Curb appeal is the first indicator whether the inside of the house is worth seeing. Why? Because a house that looks good on the outside usually looks good on the inside, too. I have never yet seen a house with a run down, ratty exterior that looks great on the inside. People are either neat or messy all over, inside and out.

That's why a homemaker should care about her home's curb appeal. The exterior of your house makes a statement about your home, just as your personal appearance makes a statement about you. The statement that your house makes, however, reflects upon your entire family, not just you. Subconsciously, most people have the attitude that *"quality people come from quality homes."* One way to give the impression of a quality home is to see that your house has a clean, tidy exterior rather than a sloppy, dirty one.

For the Christian homemaker, caring for the exterior appearance of her home is just one more way of being a good reflection of Jesus. When Jesus is Lord of our lives, He is Lord of all—including the cleanliness and orderliness of our home. No one is going to be attracted to Christianity if Christian homemakers do not maintain a positive image and high property values in our own neighborhoods. Keeping the exterior of our homes neat, clean, and well-maintained is one way of doing just that.

Every neighborhood seems to have at least one family that doesn't seem to care about the condition of its home and property. The worst offenders in any neighborhood have a house that was quite attractive and valuable when it was new, but today it's the eyesore of the subdivision. It hasn't been painted in recent history; toys and junk clutter the front porch and yard; the driveway is a mass of broken, heaved, concrete chunks splattered with black grease stains; and the lawn and flower planters are pitifully neglected and weed-infested. The inside of this home is not in much better shape. This is a classic example of a home without a homemaker—whether there is a wife there full-time or not. And a home without a homemaker is nothing more than a hotel.

But you can always tell, even by its curb appeal, when you see a home that has a real homemaker. One great example of a home that has a devoted homemaker is near my own house. This is my favorite house to look at when I stroll through the neighborhood. It's a simple, one-story house with an average-sized lot and a front-entry garage, like so many other houses in the neighborhood.

The house is well-maintained with fresh paint and clean windows. The lawn is green and well-trimmed, as are the trees and shrubs. A neat row of geraniums stands cheerily across the front of the house, and a perky potted plant hangs near the front door. Crisp curtains pull back to invite your view of a comfortable chair and sofa in one window and a pretty brass bed with a floral coverlet in the other. The total picture is one of simple hominess and happiness. This family achieved it with nothing more than a little curb appeal in the form of well-maintained neatness.

Of course, keeping a home well-maintained can at times be costly. But we must keep in mind that money spent on home maintenance is not a luxury—it is an investment in your most expensive asset. Maintaining the landscape and making needed repairs over the years can seem like an endless drain of money and energy. But remember that this money and energy will be well-spent. If you ever have to sell your home, which most Americans do on the average of every five years, all that effort will pay off. Your home will sell faster and for a higher price than it would have if you had not invested that time and money. Even if you don't plan on moving, you want to know that your property is not depreciating from neglect.

The cost of keeping a home in good condition should be an expense that you and your husband consider before buying a house, and not afterward. It's better to remain in an apartment or to purchase a condominium than it is to buy a house and then allow it to become a blight on the neighborhood. But lack of time and effort causes more neglect than lack of funds. For example, it doesn't cost a lot to plant a few flowers and put a pretty wreath on the front door. And it costs nothing at all to sweep the sidewalk and pull out weeds. But it takes a little organization to devote your time to such simple, but important, activities.

A homemaker may be the one to set the standards for the exterior appearance of her home, but she certainly shouldn't have to do all the outdoor work herself. That's why Janice talked to her husband and children about their responsibility to help with the yard work. They decided to set Saturday mornings aside and make yard work a family project. *"My husband agreed that we can teach our children more about responsibility by doing yard work with them than they could ever learn from us driving them from one entertaining activity to another on Saturdays."*

While many of their friends are taking expensive tennis lessons, going to watch questionable movies, or spending unsupervised hours at the shopping mall, Janice's children are learning the value of getting dirty and sweaty in their own backyard. While Janice sweeps the porch and washes the windows, her husband runs the lawn mower, and her children pull weeds out of the flower beds and garden. When the weather doesn't permit outside activities, they spend their time cleaning out the garage, the basement, or the attic. Then they get cleaned up and spend the afternoon together at the swimming pool, the park, or the library as their *"reward"* for getting the work done. As a result of Janice's proactive planning the work gets done, the children develop good character and family ties are strengthened.

But what if you have a husband who refuses, or is unable, to help you with the outside care of your home? Then you have three choices:

1. You can pay professionals to do the work, provided you can afford it.
2. You can allow your home to deteriorate to the point of the family in my first example.
3. You can make the best of a bad situation and, along with your children, do the work yourself without pouting, complaining, or being resentful.

Brenda took the third choice. Her husband works many hours of overtime, including Saturdays, at his new business. Instead of insisting that he spend his one free day a week doing yard work, Brenda and her children devote one afternoon a week to getting the yard in order so the family can spend a leisurely Sunday afternoon relaxing together. As a result, Brenda has not only avoided having an exhausted and resentful husband, but she's been an example to her son and daughter of going the extra mile without complaining.

Brenda is quite a contrast to someone I once knew whom I'll call Judy. Judy lived in a large, elegant home that could have been featured on the front cover of any interior decorating magazine. Judy had everything that any woman could desire, including a hard-working husband and two lovely daughters. Yet Judy never seemed satisfied.

Once, when giving me a tour of her immaculately decorated home, Judy took me out on their large deck overlooking private woods. When I remarked how lovely it all was, Judy only turned up her nose and said, *"Just look at the condition of this yard. My husband doesn't do a thing in the yard, and you just can't hire people who care enough to do a good job."*

"Then why don't you do it the way you want it?" I asked. "Oh, you must be kidding," she sniffed. "I don't like to work in the yard."

How odd, I thought, that homemaking is the only career in which one can refuse to do anything one doesn't *"like"* to do just because one doesn't like to do it. I couldn't help thinking how shocked Judy would be in any other job where she would have to do some things that she didn't like to do. As a nurse, I didn't *"like"* emptying bedpans. As a real estate agent, I didn't *"like"* doing reams of paperwork with every sale. But it was just part of the job. I wondered if Judy's husband *"liked"* doing everything in his job to provide her with such a luxurious lifestyle. But, nonetheless, Judy didn't do what Judy didn't like to do. But Judy obviously liked complaining about her husband not liking to do it.

As homemakers, the choice is up to us to set the tone for our homes depending on the attitude we take. It's up to us to decide whether we want to make home maintenance a source of family conflict or family togetherness. Whether we live in a mansion or a mobile home, we have the opportunity to make our homes an asset to the community and a positive witness for our faith. And it all begins with just a little curb appeal.

Here are some practical suggestions for achieving curb appeal at your home:

- Give the front entry to your home a welcoming appearance. Keep the porch and sidewalk swept clean. If there is room, make a small seating area with a porch swing or a couple of chairs. Some potted plants will soften and cheer the entryway. Shine the windows.
- Keep the lawn well mowed and weed-free. Trim the edges of sidewalks. Remove grass and weeds from sidewalk cracks, which is easy to do by hand after a rain.
- Don't be too proud to sweep up debris from the street in front of your home. Some neighbors may kid you, but others may notice your example and do

the same themselves. In some European countries it is commonplace to sweep the streets daily in front of your home.

- Keep flower beds clean and watered. If you don't have a green thumb, you may want to fill them in with mulch and a few shrubs. It's better to have no flowers at all than to have sad, straggly ones.
- Keep shrubs neatly trimmed to avoid that aged look that overgrown, shaggy shrubs give a home. Keep shrubs in front of windows trimmed no higher than the bottom window sill. Don't allow shrubs or trees to obstruct the view of your entryway. This deters thieves as well as making your home look nice.
- Keep trees well-trimmed, especially alongside walks. (Nothing bothers walkers more than having to duck under branches to avoid getting slapped in the face.) Lop off any branches that are growing at odd angles, and don't allow clinging vines to grow up from the base of your trees.
- Don't leave grass clippings on the street or sidewalk. (That's very tacky!)
- Keep gutters clog-free and draining well away from the foundation of your house. (This alone would solve many people's wet basement problems.)
- Keep window treatments uniform across the front of the house. One house in our neighborhood sports printed cafe curtains in one window, blinds in another window, and draperies in yet another. That home is not nearly as attractive as a similar house with simple, white Priscillas pulled back at every window.
- Use complementary colors on the exterior of your home. Avoid overly bold, bright colors—such as the purple house in our city! On the other hand, avoid the *"dull blahs"* by perking up soft, neutral colors with a touch of bolder contrast on trim work.
- Keep the garage neatly organized or keep the door closed. Most people don't want anyone peeking into their messy closets, but they don't think twice about unsightly garages.
- Keep cars parked in the garage or on the driveway whenever possible to avoid cluttered, crowded

streets. Confine their all unsightly repair projects to the garage or behind the house.
- Teach children to pick up toys and clutter from the yard at the end of the day.

We can't all have perfect homes all the time like *"Mr. Wonderful,"* the man in our neighborhood who never has a blade of grass out of place. But we can notice what improvements we need to make and set aside a regular time each week to give attention to those items. Slow, persistent progress pays off for those who wish to keep the outside of their homes in as good condition as the inside. That's real curb appeal.

ACTION ASSIGNMENTS

- *Plan a regular time for your outdoor work, whether it is for fifteen minutes every afternoon by yourself, or for a couple of hours every weekend with the whole family.*
- *Take a long walk through your neighborhood to notice the good points and bad points of each house and lawn. Determine how you can learn from others' wisdom and mistakes to improve your own home.*
- *Teach your children to enjoy physical work by including them in your gardening and yard work. Plan a family fun time as a reward for finishing the work.*

— 10 —

ORGANIZED CHILDREN?

One friend with young, lively children often moans, *"I'm going to get organized—just as soon as my kids are grown!"* I can surely sympathize with her. I remember the days win my home seemed like Toyland, I wished someone would manufacture wallpaper that was already decorated with little handprints, and life was measured by how many things I could get done between meals and diaper changes. While older women were wisely telling me, *"Enjoy them while you can; they grow up so fast,"* I was wishing they would so I could get some rest!

Today, of course, I'm telling other young mothers to *"enjoy them while you can,"* too. But I'm also telling them that you can enjoy your children more if you start now to train them to be organized. You need to keep in mind, however, that organizing children must not be done like a staff sergeant barking orders at his troops but like a shepherd leading a flock of frisky lambs. In other words, you have to allow them room to have fun along the way.

Before teaching your children how to be organized, decide exactly what you want your child to do and why. Do you want to teach your children to be confident and to master skills that they will need as adults? Or is your motive to get the kids to do the housework so Mom can play? If so, think again!

ABDICATING RESPONSIBILITY?

When my children were very young *"Women's Liberation"* was in its infancy. I read a magazine article written by a woman who claimed that she was a full-time homemaker and that she only wanted to spend her time doing things she enjoyed, such as reading novels, watching TV, and shopping with friends. She had adopted the philosophy that everyone in the family should do their own laundry, cooking, and cleaning so that she could be free to do whatever she felt like doing. If they didn't do for themselves, they did without. She took care of only herself. She rationalized that this was how to teach her children to be responsible. But by refusing to do anything for anyone but herself, this woman was teaching her children that work is bad and selfishness is good.

This article may have had had a certain surface appeal to women who were drowning in over-busyness. But I couldn't help wondering why that woman thought she should be the only person in her family who didn't have to work. Her husband had a full-time job (or she wouldn't have had the freedom to stay home), and her children had to go to school every day. She had missed the obvious point that life is work, and work is what makes life meaningful. As Solomon said in Ecclesiastes, the best way to enjoy your life is to enjoy your work.

Today women's magazines and home organization books still offer advice on how to get the rest of the family to do the housework. These publications cater to the woman who works outside the home and can't possibly do it all. The advice in these articles is usually preceded with the number one rule: *"Lower your standards. Don't expect so much."* Fortunately, as full-time homemakers, we don't have to lower our standards, and we don't have to coerce our family into doing our work for us.

But we should teach our children to be neat, clean, and orderly for their own personal benefit. A mother is a child's most important teacher, and it is our responsibility to teach our children to be responsible for themselves. Lessons in how to work happily and productively will serve our children well all their lives.

HOW TO TEACH YOUR CHILDREN

The first step in teaching children to be organized is to recognize what type of skills your child is capable of doing at his or her age. Expecting a three-year-old to make a bed without rumples or a five-year-old to clean a room perfectly is expecting the impossible. Be sure to gear all tasks age-appropriately.

The remaining steps are: patience, patience, patience! Kids will never get it right the first time, and they'll need endless repetition and reminders. But, since no one can learn well under pressure, kind perseverance must prevail over frustration. As one child said to his irate mother, *"I can't hear you when you're screaming at me!"* Children learn best when we make work into play.

To teach a child anything, one must first get him to concentrate on the task at hand. My Uncle Mitch, an avid coon hunter, knew this truth had a much broader application. Because his rotund stature prevented him from being able to navigate the rugged Oklahoma terrain, he rode a mule which he had taught to leap over creeks and fences. A local newspaper reporter interviewed my Uncle Mitch and asked him, *"How on earth do you teach a mule to jump over fences with you on its back?"*

"Well," Uncle Mitch answered sagely, *"the first step is to get its attention!"*

That's also the first step in teaching children.

When Chris teaches her preschooler any new task, she first sits down and talks to him about it. *"Matt, today Mommy is going to teach you how to put away the toys after playing outside. We must always put our toys away because we don't want them to get lost or rained on. So I will show you how I want you to put away your toys before coming back in the house."*

Then Chris shows Matt how to bring the toys into the garage and put them in the correct place.

"Look, Matt. This is your toy box where you can put all of your toys, and this is where you can park your Big Wheel. Let me show you how to put your toys away, and then you can try it."

Always demonstrate a task before asking the child to do it, no matter how simple it seems to you. Encourage him to repeat the instructions back to you and to ask questions about anything he doesn't understand. Never belittle a child's efforts, no matter how clumsy or imperfect they may be. Gently correct him and be sure to praise him for his efforts.

"That's wonderful, Matt," Chris says, *"I like the way you brought your toys into the garage. But remember to put them in this box. Why don't you try it again, honey?"*

With encouragement Matt puts away his toys without being reminded. But as soon as Chris forgets to praise him, Matt forgets to put away his toys. Rather than scolding him, Chris says, *"Matt, remember to put away your toys. Let's go outside so Mommy can see how well you do that!"*

When teaching a child to keep his room neat and orderly, give him furniture and storage boxes that are scaled down to his size. Tiny hands have a hard time manipulating big items. Imagine how overwhelmed you would feel if your kitchen counters were above your head and all the pots and utensils were twice their normal size. It would probably discourage you from cooking dinner!

When our oldest son was born, he was the first grandchild on both sides of the family. Of course, nothing was too good for this grandchild, and soon he was surrounded with the biggest and best of everything. He had the biggest red wagon, the biggest toy box, and the biggest rocking horse in our apartment complex. But he was such a little boy! His favorite toys were little wooden blocks and tiny plastic toy soldiers. They were just his size!

When teaching children to put away toys and clothing, remember to keep shelves and clothing rods low and easily accessible to your child's height. Provide them with plenty of colorful plastic crates for keeping all sorts of treasures and collectibles. Give them a place to keep artwork, rocks and other interesting things they have found. Most children are happy to help Mommy decide which special pictures they should store in their *"memory box"* and which ones they should discard to make space for new things. Explain that you must make choices because everything must fit into that box. You may want to keep a box in the basement or attic for permanent storage of such memorabilia.

If your child needs help in remembering what items belong in what place, you can tape pictures of specific items in the bottom of the container or tack a photo on the back of the shelf where he should store them. This makes it more fun for the child, like matching puzzle pieces. To help remember grooming tasks, you can also take photos of your child brushing his teeth, combing his hair, putting away his pajamas, and making his bed. Paste them onto a poster to remind him what to do each morning.

Older children can benefit from work charts with daily chores written under each day of the week. After discussing the need for organization in assigning and remembering daily tasks, your family can plan together who should do what chores, make up a chart, and post it on the refrigerator or bulletin board. Praise should be a child's daily reward for a job well done, rather than money or bribes. And punishment for not doing assigned work should be decided upon beforehand as a family. Perhaps forgetfulness will carry the penalty of an apology and doing an extra task, or helping a brother or sister do one of their jobs.

WHAT ABOUT DISCIPLINE?

Spankings can make learning and working a thing to be dreaded, rather than an enjoyable growing process. But a spanking is sometimes the most effective and loving thing a parent can do to make a lasting impression on a child's training. Paula, a homemaker with a lot of experience in teaching children, once told me, *"We only give our children spankings for three things: disobedience, dishonesty, and disrespect. Disobedience does not mean normal childish forgetfulness, but rather means willful refusal to obey us. Dishonesty is any intentional untruth, no matter how small. Disrespect is any word or action that shows rebellion against our authority as their parents."* Paula's children are among the best behaved and happiest that I have seen.

As children grow older and more mature, spankings should become a very rare event. If they happen on a frequent basis the parent needs to re-evaluate what they are doing wrong, rather than what the children are doing wrong. There may be too much rigidness or too little consistency by the parents. We've all seen cases of both just visiting the grocery store! When children reach school age and are old enough to remember their indiscretions without immediate action, it's a good time to transfer any spanking responsibilities to your husband. Physical punishment becomes more emotionally stressful for a mother and her child as the child grows older. I can tell you from experience that it's impossible to spank a child who towers over you!

My husband once told me, *"When I grew up, Dad was the disciplinarian and Mom was the one who nurtured. If I did something wrong, I knew Mom would tell Dad. He would give me a good talking to or a spanking if it was necessary. It made me respect both of them."* Once our children were past the baby stage, I was happy to turn that job over to him.

SOW GOOD SEED

The Bible conveys a spiritual truth that applies to every parent. *"Be not deceived; God is not mocked: for whatsoever a man sows, that shall he also reap."* (Galatians 6:7). Most of us who are able to choose a stay-at-home career do so primarily for the sake of raising and nurturing our children properly. We want to be sure that the seed sown in our children will be good seed. We don't wish to entrust that important seed planting to strangers at daycare centers. Our teaching and example insures that the seed we plant in our tender, young children will last a lifetime. Seed will inevitably sprout and bear fruit, whether for good or for evil. This involves every area of your child's life—manners, organization and his morality.

God's Word emphasizes the responsibility to sow good seed in our children and to consider children a blessing from Him. This cuts against the grain of the current theory that children are influenced ninety percent by genetics and environment and only ten percent by parental influence. And it directly opposes society's attitude that children are more a burden than a blessing.

For that reason, we must be mindful of the seed we sow in our children's lives. We must remember that seeds of home-centeredness are sown by encouraging home-centered activities. We must also remember that seeds of rebellion and evil are sown by exposing a child to literature, television, movies, music, or people with ungodly values. What a child sees, he will emulate.

For that reason many parents have chosen to prohibit anything from their homes that does not honor God or edify their children. They prohibit any literature, television, movies, or toys that glorify unnecessary violence or immorality. They refuse to allow their children to make idols of rock stars who promote drugs, violence, and rebellion. They also ban attitudes of materialism, snobbishness, and prejudice from their homes. They do this in obedience to God's Word, which says, *"Neither shalt thou bring an abomination into thine house, lest thou be a cursed thing like it,"* (Deuteronomy 7:26, KJV). Many young people today have, indeed, become *"a cursed thing,"* like the ungodly things their parents have allowed into their homes.

When our sons were in elementary school, they wanted to start a beer can collection like their friends were doing. I said no to that, telling them that they could collect soda cans instead. A short time later they wanted to know if they could buy a record album by a heavy metal rock group, like their friends had. I asked them to look at the evil looking men on the album cover and consider whether that is the kind of person they wanted to become. As they grew older we had to establish firm limits on movies we permitted them to see, all in spite of what their friends were doing. That wasn't easy, but it was perhaps one thing that helped prevent them from becoming drug addicts like many of their friends.

Liberal psychology tells us that this is censorship and that we should allow our children to grow up without the influence of our values so that they can *"decide for themselves"* when they are older. God's Word tells us that it's our responsibility as parents to protect our children from evil, and to *"train up a child in the way he should go, even when he is old he will not depart from it"* (Proverbs 22:6).

We once moved out of a neighborhood due primarily to the bad influences of several of the neighborhood children, and a few years later we learned that our children's playmates who did all those *"normal things that kids do today"* had become involved heavily with drugs and immorality. Their homes had become unhappy war zones instead of places of refuge from the world. We thanked God for giving us the courage to ban such unhealthy influences from our home from the very beginning.

In his book <u>Set the Trumpet to Thy Mouth</u>, David Wilkerson many years ago wisely wrote, *"There is enough hell for [our children] to face outside the home. The home should be a holy, sanctified sanctuary, a place of rest and peace from the corruption of the age—and a place where Jesus is real and the Holy Spirit ever present."*

Of course, the strongest influence in our children's lives is that of our own personal example. That's why it's important for us as homemakers to present an example of kindness, orderliness, and godliness in all aspects of our lives. There are no guarantees that our children will turn out exactly as we wish they would, no matter how *"perfect"* we may try to be as their parents. But we are obliged to do our best with the children God has given us for as long as we have them. The rest is up to God, and to our children themselves.

When we attended the college graduation of our oldest son, one of his apartment neighbors, who liked and befriended him during his years at college, attended the ceremony with our family. She repeatedly said, *"You must have done something right when you raised that boy!"* Finally I replied, *"Well, I guess we will take the liberty of accepting your compliment. But if he had turned out badly, it would have been all his fault!"*

Not all of us were born natural *"earth mothers"* who knew instinctively how to do everything right—certainly not I! But as we mature in Christ, He leads us through every difficulty and mistake for His name's sake. Even in child-rearing it is true: *"There is therefore now no condemnation for those who are in Christ Jesus."* (Romans 8:1) That's a good scripture to remember at the end of a frustrating day.

To teach a child discipline and organization, we must be very consistent in enforcing our rules. We need to have as few rules as possible so we are not constantly correcting our children for things that don't matter. One teacher told me, *"Consistency and discipline walk hand in hand. You can't have one without the other. If you make a rule, you must always follow through on it. If you decide it was a bad rule, explain to the child why you are changing your mind so he won't be confused."* If we considered all the effort it takes to enforce every rule, we would probably be more prudent about the rules we make. Isn't it better to have fewer rules and more consistent follow-through?

The most important reason we strive to teach our children to be organized is not to have an immaculate house but rather to help develop their character. Just as the military requires cleanliness and organization to develop discipline for more important duties, we teach our children to be organized about little things in the hope that one day they will be equipped to be responsible in much larger matters.

One day, when your children are grown and gone, you'll have time for a perfect house. What matters now is not the house, but the home; and not the children's duties, but the children. To every mother of young children who worries herself unnecessarily with trying to do too much, I can only say, *"There is an appointed time for everything. And there is a time for every event under heaven."* (Ecclesiastes 3:1)

If you're feeling overburdened by your responsibilities to church, school, and community feel free to drop out of volunteering for a while. You can fulfill your duties as a *"good citizen"* when your kids are grown. The noblest task you can do for God, for your community, and for your country is to raise good citizens today. If that's all you accomplish in your lifetime, you will have accomplished more than most *"famous"* people! Take it from one who knows, and *"enjoy them while you can!"*

ACTION ASSIGNMENTS

- *Evaluate what age-appropriate duties you want to teach to your children.*
- *Call a family conference and discuss why you wish to teach responsibilities to your children. Have them help you in suggesting what duties they should assume. Decide in advance what penalty will be incurred for failure to complete each duty.*
- *Post a "Duty Sheet" for older children. Take photos and make a poster of "Things To Do" for younger children.*
- *Heap on the praise and encouragement for positive efforts. Be consistent on penalties for disobedience.*
- *Post "The Rules of Our Home" for a permanent reminder to everyone of expected behavior. Discuss at a family meeting what each rule should be, and feel free to re-evaluate those rules as the children mature.*

11

HOW TO HANDLE A HUSBAND

In the musical Camelot, King Arthur asks a wise little wizard named Merlin the age-old question, *"How do you handle a woman?"* Many homemakers today wish they had Merlin around to give them the magical answer to *"How do you handle a husband?"*

"My husband is such a sloppy person! All I ever do is clean up after him," is a frequent complaint from wives who are tired of picking up a trail of shoes, neckties, and underwear from the floor.

"My husband is a sports addict," complain many others. *"He sits glued to every football, baseball, and basketball game on television. As soon as one season is over, the other has already begun. How can I ever get him to pay attention to me or help out around the house?"*

Another wife groans, *"My husband is a workaholic. He spends more time at the office than he does at home. The children are beginning to wonder who he is!"*

Husband problems are innumerable. Fortunately, however, we don't have to rely on a fictitious magician for our answers. We have a much better marriage guide, which was written by the One who created marriage in the first place.

FOLLOWING GOD'S ORDER

In the book of *Genesis* we find Adam in the Garden of Eden (a perfect place, even neater than Hawaii) naming all the animals, dining on luscious fruits, and best of all, never having to clock in at the office. Don't you think Adam would have been perfectly happy in such a Utopian existence? But no! Even his Creator said, *"It is not good for the man to be alone. I will make him a helper suitable for him."* (Genesis 2:18)

So God created Eve for Adam, and woman for man. Too often we have the wrong impression that man was created to be a helpmeet to woman! Ever since that day there have been problems between the sexes. (Remember the apple?)

Fortunately, however, God gave us the rest of the Bible, which is filled with Holy Spirit inspired ideas for getting along together. These ideas worked well until recently. That's when so-called *"Women's Liberation"* came into vogue and discarded God's plan for marriage. As a result, today nearly one out of every two marriages ends in divorce. So it might behoove us to re-examine God's plan for *"how to handle a husband"* rather than the world's plan.

We could boil the Scriptures down to this simple formula: *"Wives, treat your husbands as reverently and respectfully as you would treat the Lord Jesus Christ. Have a submissive, rather than a defiant, attitude. Let your beauty be more than just a lovely appearance, but rather an inward gentleness and quietness of spirit, which is precious to God"* (paraphrased from 1 Peter 3:1-6; Ephesians 5:22-33).

Regarding our role at home, Titus 2:3-5 tells us, *"Older women likewise are to be reverent in their behavior, not malicious gossips, nor enslaved to much wine, teaching what is good, that they may encourage the young women to love their husbands, to love their children, to be sensible, pure, workers at home, kind, being subject to their own husbands, that the word of God may not be dishonored."*

Did you ever stop to think that a Christian's disobedience to any of those commands causes the word of God to be dishonored? It gives those in the world another reason to mock God's word and call us hypocrites. But many Christian women balk at being under the protective headship of their husbands because they don't like the big no-no word *"submit"*! It rubs us the wrong way, especially in our culture of individuality and independence.

But, interpreted correctly, submission is not a word that means *"slavery,"* but rather *"servant."* A slave is a person who serves because she has to, out of compulsion. A servant is one who serves because she chooses to, out of love. Submission is also a way of letting God deal with your husband instead of having your husband fight against you. If you tell your husband that you disagree with him on a particular decision, and then argue and sulk, your actions will provoke him to feel defensive and justified in his stance. But if you explain your point of view and then defer to his decision in the end, trusting God to guide him—that puts him on the spot! As one pastor succinctly put it, *"Submission is ducking so God can hit your husband."*

Scripture gives us good examples of wives who practiced God's successful principles. Some of my favorites are Priscilla, who faithfully helped her husband with their tent making business and functioned as his teammate in ministering the gospel to others (see Acts 18:26), and Sarah, who Scripture tells us, *"obeyed Abraham, calling him Lord."* The Bible also says, *"and you have become her children if you do what is right without being frightened by any fear."* (1 Peter 3:6) As long as you're submitting to your husband *"as is fitting in the Lord"* (meaning not in any sinful thing), you need not be afraid of the results. (See Colossians 3:18)

But my favorite wife is the godly woman in Proverbs 31, of whom it is said, *"The heart of her husband trusts in her, and he will have no lack of gain. She does him good and not evil all the days of her life"* (Proverbs 31:11,12). As a result of her faithfulness, her husband praises her, saying, *"Many daughters have done nobly, but you excel them all!"* (Proverbs 31:29)

WHAT EVERY HUSBAND CRAVES

All the successful wives in God's Word gave their husband something that every husband covets more than money, fame--or even sex! Most husbands are starving for it. And it's something that guarantees a happy husband. What is this secret ingredient? It's spelled R-E-S-P-E-C-T.

The Bible says, *"Let each individual among you also love his own wife even as himself; and let the wife see to it that she respect her husband."* (Ephesians 5:33) Why doesn't the Bible say, *"and let the wife see to it that she loves her husband,"* too? I believe that's because the best way we can love our husbands is to treat them with respect. No husband receiving disrespect can ever feel loved.

Respect means never belittling, nagging, or being rude. Respect means never revealing your husband's flaws to friends or family, or making him appear like your oppressor, so that you can get sympathy. Any wife who rolls her eyes in disrespect is signaling a doomed marriage. Respect implies courtesy, kindness, and admiration. Respect is not making your husband drive a car with a personalized license plate that reads *"DUM-DUM,"* like one I saw a man driving. And it's not putting a bumper sticker on your car that says, *"Husband and Dog Lost: Reward for Dog."* They might seem funny, but making the man of the house the butt of jokes is never edifying to him. Godly humor never sacrifices someone else's respect. Every husband should be treated with respect, if for no other reason than for the position he holds as a husband. A man is more motivated to behave in a manner deserving respect if his wife treats him respectfully. And a wife who treats her husband respectfully is more likely to be respected in return.

Treating your husband with respect includes nurturing him. If you think you need to nurture only your children, think again! Husbands hide tender, little-boy hearts deep inside and will soak up nurturing like thirsty flowers soak up the gentle rain. If you don't believe it, just try giving your husband a few hugs, kisses, and sweet words tonight. Bring him a little snack, treat him like a guest in his own home, and talk to him as tenderly as you would to a young child—and watch him bloom! Every day stop to ask yourself, *"What have I done to nurture my husband today?"*

AN UNGODLY WOMAN'S INFLUENCE

Besides many good examples, the Bible also records the example of an ungodly woman who did everything opposed to God's plan for a wife. Her name was Jezebel. She led her husband Ahab, the king of Israel, into Baal worship. Baal worshipers disgusted God because they killed their children as sacrifices, among other things. God states that He will bring calamity upon those who worship Baal *"because they have forsaken Me and have . . . filled this place with the blood of the innocent and have built the high places of Baal to burn their sons in the fire as burnt offerings to Baal, a thing which I never commanded or spoke of, nor did it ever enter My mind."* (Jeremiah 19:4,5)

Jezebel had several other bad qualities, too. She was a murderess, a manipulator, and an enemy of God's servants. The Bible says, *"Surely there was no one like Ahab who sold himself to do evil in the sight of the Lord, because Jezebel his wife incited him."* (1 Kings 21:25) Her life is a chilling example of the power that a woman can have over her husband for evil.

Sadly, today many women have become infected by the same spirit that drove Jezebel. Rather than walking in obedience to God's Word, they choose to embrace the values and attitudes of the world. They care more about what they think is right than what God says is right. In short, they are women who choose to have a Jezebel spirit rather than the spirit of the godly wife in Proverbs 31, or Abraham's wife Sarah, who obeyed her husband and called him Lord.

Jezebel is loud, crude, and manipulative. She dresses to attract attention and provoke sexual lust. She lacks manners and social graces. She even rules over her husband. She is motivated only by her own self-interest.

Sarah, on the other hand, is quiet, gentle and truthful. She dresses in a feminine, attractive and modest manner. She is also mannerly and graceful. She is motivated to honor her husband by making him look as good as possible to everyone. She keeps his flaws to herself, just as she wishes to be treated.

GOD'S MANDATE FOR HUSBANDS

"So what about my husband?" you ask. *"What does Scripture say he should do?"*

Here's a simple scriptural formula for husbands: *"Husbands, love your wives just as sacrificially as Christ loved the church. Protect and care for her, sheltering her from the cares of the world. Treat her as you would treat your own body, for you are now one flesh. Prefer her above all others."* (Paraphrased from Ephesians 5:25-32)

Regarding a husband's role in the home, scripture bluntly states, *"But if anyone does not provide for his own, and especially for those of his household, he has denied the faith, and is worse than an unbeliever."* (1 Timothy 5:8)

This obviously puts the financial burden on the husband, leaving his wife free to manage the home and nurture the children. It also implies that the wife should not put unnecessary, frivolous financial demands on her husband so that he is able to fulfill his obligation in this area. In this day of inflation and high taxes, husband and wife must work as a team if they want to keep the wife in the home—and it is work! He works hard to bring the money home, and she works hard to make it stretch as far as possible by being industrious and frugal. They both teach their children to do the same.

Obviously, it helps the husband fulfill his scriptural roles if the wife fulfills hers, and visa-versa. A man is not motivated to work hard and be loving for a lazy, complaining, self-centered woman. And it's very difficult for a woman to have a sweet, submissive attitude toward a man who is demanding and controlling. This is when outside counseling may be very helpful in helping a couple see their own behavior from the perspective of a non-biased observer.

MOTIVATING YOUR SPOUSE

If you're having problems with your husband—and who doesn't from time to time?—the best way to motivate him to act the way you want him to is for you to act the way he wants you to. The Golden Rule, *"Do unto others as you would have them do unto you,"* really does bring results.

Is your husband driving you to distraction by throwing his dirty clothes on the floor and leaving a trail of clutter behind him? First, try to politely (as opposed to accusingly) let him know that you would appreciate his thoughtfulness in this area. Gentle truthful reminders, rather than nagging, help.

Second, provide your husband with easy access to a clothes hamper, and let him know where things belong. (Sometimes husbands don't realize that. This helped my husband immensely, much to my surprise.)

Finally, if all else fails, see if you can pick up after him without complaining (to yourself or to others) as an offering of thankfulness to the Lord for providing you with your husband. I read a touching anecdote years ago about a woman who was visiting a friend. As they sat talking in the kitchen, the friend's husband tracked mud across her spotless floor. The visitor remarked to the wife, *"His boots certainly do bring the dirt in."* *"Yes,"* the smiling wife replied as she got up to get the broom. *"But they bring him in, too."* This couple had been married for fifty-four years, and you can see why. It is just another way to honor your husband to pick up after him.

Does your husband sit for hours on end in front of the television, watching sports or sci-fi movies? Once again, you might try telling him how you feel about this. See if you can compromise so that he watches less TV and you spend more time doing other things with him. Make sure he's not watching television to escape from you or from problems he can't deal with.

See if you can encourage him to find other means of relaxation. If all else fails, just consider the time your husband spends in front of the television to be free time for you, too. Find a hobby you can enjoy while he's being a couch potato.

But be sure you don't begrudge your husband a fair amount of time doing whatever he enjoys, whether it is watching TV, golfing, fishing, or any other non-harmful activity. One woman I know complains bitterly about the few weekends her husband spends away on hunting trips. *"I need him here to help me with the kids. I'm with them all the time, and he should help me with them when he isn't at work,"* she says. This woman forgets that she doesn't have to contend with his job and his boss every day. Husbands need some time off, too. Men need time alone and time spent with friends as much as women do. A relaxed, happy husband is a lot easier to live with than one who isn't.

If you can't draw your husband's attention away from his hobby, try something novel—join him! I know one wife who enjoys duck hunting and another who thinks it's great fun to stalk deer. When Jane's husband bought a hot air balloon, she took pilot's lessons right along with him.

Another way to get your husband to pay attention to you is to be available. Use the hours your husband is at work to do your housework. Then use the hours he is home to be with him, rather than to do the ironing or paint the bathroom. Housework requires fewer hours if we're properly organized. Making your evening hours family time can have a major impact on family togetherness.

I know of one woman who complains to anyone who will listen about her husband and her marriage. But it's no wonder they enjoy no partnership. She attends the following activities alone: Sunday, church; Monday evening, aerobics class; Tuesday evening, book club; Wednesday evening, church again; and Thursday evening, yoga. That leaves two days a week in which to try to build a relationship with her husband. I believe the devil would rather see us spending all our time in church or anywhere else if it will keep us from spending time with our husband and children.

Being an on-the-go wife and mother can add a lot of stress to your family, but the workaholic husband can be a difficult problem, too. This man is compulsively obsessed with his career and *"getting ahead"* to the point of neglecting his family. He leaves his wife alone to deal with all the weighty decisions at home and provides very little role-modeling for the children.

If you're unable to communicate your needs as a wife and mother in having more time with your husband, you might try Christian counseling or a couple's retreat. He needs to understand that providing financially for his family is not his sole responsibility as a husband and father. He needs to learn scriptures that show his responsibility to teach and discipline his children, as well as to love and cherish his wife. Your husband needs to learn to relax and enjoy life himself.

PUT IT IN PERSPECTIVE

But when it comes right down to it there is very little anyone can do to change someone else. It is much more likely that we can change ourselves, and accept others where they are.

If your husband is a workaholic, avoid the temptation to argue and complain. Provide a home environment that is pleasant in the hope that your husband will be enticed to spend more time there. But if he proves to be an incorrigible workaholic, accept the good (he is providing well for you) and spend your time alone constructively. Rather than seeking solace in soap operas or destructive affairs, turn your loss to gain by spending your extra time managing your home well or doing volunteer work for the needy. (Nothing takes your mind off your problems like helping those with worse ones.)

I once read, *"We cannot make people over. Our business is to make ourselves better and others happy, and that is enough to keep us busy."* How true. There is also a wise proverb that says, *"Before you marry, keep both eyes open; after you marry, shut one."*

It may not always be easy to be married to your husband, but few worthwhile things in life are ever easy. The alternative, divorce, is certainly not easy, either. No wonder God hates divorce.

"The divorce epidemic not only has devastated childhood, it has brought financial ruin to millions of women," stated a White House report on the American family. *"Divorce reform was supposed to be a panacea for women trapped in bad marriages. It has trapped many of them in poverty."* They should have also added that divorce traps the divorced husband and father in poverty, too. Many homeless men on the street are there due to child support and alimony payments that they simply could not afford, demanded by over-zealous courts. In those cases everyone lost, and lives were destroyed.

Facing problems like that should put picking up a pair of dirty socks in proper perspective. To maintain a happy marriage, we must avoid the temptation to make mountains out of molehills. We can do that best by not complaining about things that don't really matter. One British saying goes, *"Faults are thick where love is thin."*

That brings us back to old Merlin, who gave his sage advice to King Arthur in Camelot. If it were revised for the female gender it would go: *"How to handle a husband? Listen well, and I'll tell you, dear. The way to handle a husband is to love him. Simply love him, merely love him, love him, love him!"*

Now, isn't that just what Jesus would say?

ACTION ASSIGNMENTS

- *Read the Scriptures regarding marriage. Pray for God's guidance on how you can improve your marriage through applying His Word to your specific situation.*
- *Think of ways for providing more enjoyable "together" activities with your husband. Arrange your schedule so that your evenings can be spent with your husband and children, rather than doing housework.*
- *Practice nurturing your husband. Find ways that you can minister love, caring, and tenderness to the secret, little-boy heart hidden within him.*
- *When tempted to be resentful of your imperfect husband, put it in perspective. Are you better off in your situation than the divorced mother next door? Most likely, if you knew her whole situation, you are.*

—— 12 ——

FEEDING YOUR FAMILY

"The worst thing about being a homemaker is having to fix breakfast, lunch and dinner every day; day in and day out," sighed Maggie. *"It's an endless, thankless task. And it seems that the more time I spend trying to make a new and different meal, the more complaints I get about it."*

I knew just what she meant. I'll never forget when I was a young bride, trying to learn to cook things that pleased my husband. He like chili, so I consulted several different recipes in an attempt to find one that he liked. After I spent hours simmering some fancy concoction of ingredients from scratch, he would sit down, take a careful taste, and say, *"Well, it's okay—but it just doesn't taste like my mother's chili."*

Finally I just gave up and bought a can of chili, heated it on the stove and served it. I thought it might do him good to appreciate the difference. This time he took a bite, swallowed, and his eyes lit up. *"Wow! That tastes just like Mom's!"*

Today I can laugh at that story, but at the time I didn't think it was funny. But the more I got to know my mother-in-law the more I learned from her that doing things the hard way isn't always necessary—especially in the kitchen.

When it comes to getting meals on the table the homemaker has a choice; she can look at this duty as a dreary chore, or she can look at it as an opportunity for creative ministry to her family. The disorganized homemaker will probably look at it as the former; the organized homemaker is more likely to approach it as the latter. Organization makes all the difference in how successful we are at providing healthy, enjoyable meals for our family.

To be organized in this area we need to concentrate on several areas:
- Organization of the Kitchen
- Menu Planning
- Shopping
- Meal Preparation

Let's look at each area in detail. By following these practical tips you won't have to dread feeding your family.

ORGANIZATION IN THE KITCHEN

If you were a famous cook, such as Julia Childs or Martha Stewart, would you be satisfied with the organization of your kitchen? You probably don't have, or need, the large assortment of equipment that those women have. Perhaps you dream of having a large, up-to-date kitchen like they do. But one thing that you can have just as much as any famous cook is a well-organized, clean, smoothly functioning kitchen.

Since feeding your family every day is just as important as cooking for books and TV shows, you need an organized kitchen just as much as they do. And, as a busy wife and mother, your time and personal satisfaction are just as valuable as theirs. But, just like Julia and Martha, you alone can organize your kitchen in a manner that is just right for you. So, taking into account your own kitchen layout and your personal cooking habits, begin by taking a critical look at your kitchen. And the two important organizational tips that will streamline your kitchen (or any other room) are:

1. Get rid of everything you don't use.
2. Group similar kinds of items together.

Going through one cabinet and drawer at a time, pull out everything in there and before cleaning that space and putting everything back in, remove all freeloaders that take up space without paying their way. If you've had that fondue pot for ten years only to dust it annually and put it back on the shelf, put it in a large box labeled, *"Get Out of My Kitchen!"* Put any and every item that you don't use into that box. Then give that box away or put it in a garage sale or sell it all on eBay. Just make it go away, never to return. If you haven't used it in a year or two you never will.

The only exception to this should be items that you never use only because they were so poorly stored that they have been too difficult to find and get out, so that you forgot you even owned them. Now that you have made more space by throwing out items that you don't need or want, put those seldom-used tools in a more convenient location. For instance, if you never use your food processor because it's stashed away in a deep, dark corner near the stove, you need to find it a better home. A food processor is a valuable tool for any cook. Wash it and make a place for it where it can be easily retrieved.

Do not keep equipment that does what another piece of equipment can do. When my blender broke I didn't need to replace it because I found that my food processor could do everything that I used it for. Several small appliances that duplicate the same job may be stealing space in your kitchen.

Get rid of equipment that you don't use because it's too much work to clean after each use, or because it is just too specialized. Do you really need that hot dog cooker that your sister gave you? Do you ever really use that waffle iron? Or that fritter fryer? Or noodle maker? If you haven't used it in the past year you probably won't miss it. If you do want to use it, make it more accessible.

Keep in mind that the fewer things you own, the less those things own you. Make it your goal to see how little, rather than how much, you can get by with. How many pots and pans do you have? How many burners are on your stove? If you have only four burners, do you really need thirty pots and pans? Ask yourself such questions as you search through your kitchen.

Once you've finished your search-and-destroy mission it's time to rearrange what remains. The key to quickly finding items is to group similar items together. For example, use each shelf in your food pantry for a different type of item. Perhaps the top shelf could be used to store paper and plastic items, because they are lightweight and easy to lift in and out from a high spot. The next shelf could be used to store baking items, like flour, sugar, etc. Then the next could be used for boxed items. And the next shelf for canned or bottled items, and so forth. That way you will know right where to put things when you unload the groceries, where to find them when you need them, and you can tell at a glance what you need when you prepare your shopping list.

Grouping similar items makes organization easy, and sub grouping makes it even easier. Organize your canned goods into neat rows, like in the grocery store, so you know whatever item is in front is the same behind it. Stack a row of canned string beans, a row of canned corn, a row of peas or soup, from front to back on the shelf. Group cake mixes in a row on the boxed goods shelf, then boxes of pasta, etc. If you have a lot of spices arrange them alphabetically so you don't have to read every label.

Follow the same idea with your storage cabinets. Keep all metal pots and pans in one cabinet. Group all plastic containers in another cabinet. Store all china together in one cabinet, all glasses in another, etc. If you have the room you can store all of your baking items in one baking-center area, like under a center island.

Organize your each kitchen drawer the same way, with one drawer for flatware, another for cooking utensils and gadgets, and another for towels and potholders. Maybe you have a drawer for paper, pens, coupons, scissors and such. Maybe you can use a large crock next to your stove just for long handled cooking spoons and spatulas. And find a place to keep your cookbooks all in one location.

Organize your freezer shelves the same way, with one shelf for meat, one for frozen vegetables, and one for frozen snacks, or however it makes sense to you. Do the same thing in your refrigerator shelving. What a difference it will make when it is time to cook and you can actually see what you have to work with.

If you don't quite have enough space you can hang large pots and pans from a hanging baker's rack or hooks under the stove hood. Just have the minimum amount of clutter on your countertops. Nothing is as dreary as over cluttered counters with appliances and piles crammed shoulder to shoulder like people in a crowded elevator. Allow only those items that are used on a daily basis, such as the toaster or can opener, to sit on top of the counters, allowing clean, open workspace. Put everything possible behind closed doors.

Next clean off the top of the refrigerator. That makes it much more attractive and easier to dust once a week. If possible, remove magnets and clutter from your refrigerator door. That is the first thing that needs to go whenever anyone is putting their house on the market because it is so unattractive. Find a nice pegboard area for displaying family photos and notices. Less is more is as true when decorating a kitchen as in any other room of the house.

MENU PLANNING

One way to avoid monotonous meals and last minute panic at dinnertime is to plan your meals every week prior to shopping. Many women don't plan their menus ahead of time because they are overwhelmed by the thought of searching through cookbooks and clippings to get menu ideas. So why not just make up a notebook or recipe box full of your family's favorites and just choose from there, only adding or removing those recipes whenever you have the time and the inclination? Don't worry about planning new and elaborate meals when you plan ahead; go with what you already know works well.

You can even make up a plan for a week's worth of menus that you save and rotate from week to week so you don't grow tired of them. My best friend in high school hated meals at home because her mother had just one weekly meal plan that they repeated every single week. That is not appealing! But you could probably make up four to eight different weeks' worth of menus without your family growing tired of those meals. Just put them on a chart in a notebook and pull out a ready-made weeks' worth of menus, with recipes, and you can easily make your shopping list from that.

And during the week you might want to have a different type of meal each night of the week. Maybe you want to have Meatless Mondays, Italian Tuesdays, Mexican Wednesdays, Chinese Thursdays, Fish on Fridays, Appetizer Night on Saturdays, and Soup on Sundays. Having a different theme each night of the week provides variety and makes choosing recipes easier. You can even get the children involved in meal planning.

Find a set day of each week to sit down and plan your meals, check the grocery ads and clip coupons, and write your grocery list. Clean out the refrigerator as you go through it to see what you need, throwing out anything that looks old and unfamiliar. Straighten pantry shelves as you check them. All of these activities work so well together that it makes sense to do them at the same time. What a pleasure it will be when you arrive home to put away the groceries in your clean, organized kitchen!

Another very good idea is to insist on family dinners together at night. Life has become so complicated with people running here and there for sports and meetings that some families rarely ever sit down at the same table at the same time. That is not the way to encourage family togetherness. Make it a high priority to prepare excellent meals and have the family actually show up and be there. After all, your family is what meals are all about.

GROCERY SHOPPING

Ideally, the organized homemaker never grocery shops with small children, but instead leaves them at home with her Fairy Godmother. But for those who who live in the real world there are a few helpful tips that may help to prevent you from becoming one of those mothers having grocery store melt-downs (either yours or your children's.) Plan ahead well so you can limit the time that you actually have to spend shopping. Keep in mind that the younger children are the less time away from home they can tolerate well. Plan your trip to the store for a time when your children are rested and not hungry. Allow them to bring along a favorite toy or book if they wish.

Be sure to explain any rules to them before you leave the house, reinforce the rules prior to entering the store, and be firm in enforcing those rules. The rules may include, *"No cookies or candy,"* or *"no getting out of the shopping cart,"* or *"no asking for anything while we shop,"* or whatever you find that works for you. Do not allow infractions. If they disobey, take them back to the car and reinforce the rules before taking them back inside. Never spank or punish a child publicly. Humiliation destroys a child.

Getting through the store without a scene in front of the candy at the checkout counter is a challenge for any mother of small children. I suggest you resort to bribery. (Every grandmother is an expert at that!) Promise a reward for good behavior. Allow them to choose one item which they can have *after* you go through the checkout. Or see if your store has a no-candy checkout lane.

As the children get older they can actually become an asset in grocery shopping if you give them part of your shopping list. They can find things for you and throw them into the cart.

Plan your grocery shopping for the same day each week according to your weekly schedule. Decide whether you want to shop at one store or whether it is worth it to you to hunt bargains at several different locations depending upon your schedule, your energy level and your budget, and upon the ages of your children.

Learn to shop frugally. Frugal doesn't mean *"cheap."* It just means never wasting anything, including money. Every penny you save is tax-free to you, and it's better in your pocket than in someone else's. In my early married years I had no choice but to make a very tiny food budget last for a whole week. I remember the hot tears of embarrassment on my cheeks whenever I would get in the car after leaving the grocery store when I had to put something back because I didn't have the cash to pay for everything I had chosen. I learned to count in my head as I picked up things so I knew I could pay for it by the time I checked out—a habit I still have today.

I also learned how to get three meals out of one chicken to feed four of us. I learned how to put together a meal from what seems to be nothing in the cupboard. To this day I can't bear to throw out a perfectly good turkey carcass any more than I can bear to discard a small piece of quilting fabric. Turning seemingly worthless leftover into something of value is an art and a joy.

A friend once told me, somewhat critically, *"You are the most frugal person I have ever known."* I chose to take that as a compliment. As long as I am generous with others and I don't confuse *"cheap"* with *"frugal"*, I am quite satisfied to be accused of being frugal. How can you keep from becoming too parsimonious? Be always on the lookout for ways to bless others out of your however-limited abundance. Whenever you have guests see if you can send them home with some small gift. Give a friend having a hard time a gift of cookies or a meal. Then watch how God will bless you in return, when you least expect it. One of the ways He will bless you is to help you discover new ideas on how to stretch your budget. Feeding your family wisely is one of the best ways you can find to do that.

Oddly enough, the more healthy, fresh foods you prepare, the less expensive your foods cost. Prepared foods, fast foods and snacks are what eat up the budget much faster than fresh fruits and vegetables and home baked items. It cost much less to eat well than to eat fast foods from the drive-through. And being at home full time rather than working at an outside job all day frees you up with the time to do that if you are organized.

If you can make the time to use coupons don't carry the whole newspaper full of ads. Clip just the ones you want in advance, or use a fancy couponing notebook, and don't buy anything you won't really use just because it's on sale. *If you don't need it, it isn't a bargain.* However, if it is on sale and you also have coupons and you will use it any time before expiration, by all means buy it.

Also, do keep a lot of extra non-perishable food and water on hand in case of emergencies. We just had a huge hurricane on the east coast and it was sad to see people in the New York area within three days rooting desperately through dumpsters for food. If you don't think a natural disaster or act of terrorism could happen in your neighborhood you have your head in the sand. Prepare and hope you never need it. But if a disaster happens you do not want to be one of the people out there fighting for food. Be part of the solution rather than part of the problem. Store enough for you and a neighbor if need be.

When grocery shopping, never go on an empty stomach. That alone will save you a lot of money on impulse buys. Make a list and stick to it. Remember that the *"real"* food is located on the outside walls of the store—the fresh produce, the meat and dairy products. The dangerous, and expensive, section is inside where you find the potato chips, the dips, the cookies and little gremlin cereals, etc., all in that inner costly section. They will tempt you to abandon your shopping plan, your budget and your diet! Tread carefully there after first shopping the outside walls and filling your cart with fresh, nutritious foods.

While standing in the checkout line I enjoy *"free reading"* if the line is slow, perusing magazine that I put back before taking my items out of the cart. I also sometimes enjoy looking at the other people and what they are buying. Have you ever noticed how much they match? The slim, muscular woman in her yoga pants has a cart full of fresh fruits and veggies, yogurt, skim milk and a few lean meats. The fat fellow with the suspenders has a load of beer and chips. The rotund lady with the pudgy children has a cart loaded down with ice cream, cheese puffs, donuts and frozen pizzas. And a few bags of candy bars. Have you ever noticed that people who eat lots of donuts actually start looking like donuts? Soft, round and pale? I try to keep that in mind as my mouth waters as I pass the Krispy Kreme dispenser! (Not always successfully.)

Once you carry your groceries to the car place the frozen items in a Styrofoam cooler that you keep there to keep them cold. That way you don't have to rush home if you need to make another stop or two.

When you get home and put away the groceries that is a good time to prepare some of your foods. Wash and dry fruits and vegetables. You can go ahead and chop carrot and celery sticks and put them in plastic bags. Did you know that Romaine lettuce will last several days if you wash and dry it, then wrap it in a dishtowel or paper towels and then put it inside a plastic bag? Or go ahead and tear up your cleaned lettuce and salad veggies and put them into containers, ready to serve. Later just put a handful on each plate and add chopped tomatoes and dressing at the last minute.

It might also be a good time to go ahead and brown some ground beef with onions, salt and pepper for use later in the week. Place the drained meat in storage bags and pop them into the freezer, ready for use in recipes later in the week. How fast it is to prepare Sloppy Joes, spaghetti or casseroles when the meat is already prepared. Divide chicken parts into plastic bags according to what you plan to make with them. Throw wings and backs into a large bag for later use in soups. By the time you finish putting away your groceries, preparing foods and cleaning up the kitchen you are well on the way to a great week of meals for your family.

MEAL PREPARATION

The way to take the drudgery to meal prep is simple: plan ahead and stick to your plan. You have already done most of the work. Step one was to have a well-organized, clean kitchen. Step two was to select your week's menus in advance. Step three was shopping efficiently once a week, avoiding extra time-and-budget consuming trips to the store. And step four was pre-prepping our foods as you put them away. By now you have completed most of the work of making dinner!

Just think about what you are preparing for tomorrow night's dinner while you are cleaning up tonight's meal. That is the time to take frozen items out of the freezer to thaw in the refrigerator. Think about when you want to actually prepare the food tomorrow. Is it a slow-cooker meal that you need to put together in the morning, or will it be last-minute tacos? You might want to set out the slow cooker to remind you to get it together in the morning. What can you prepare early in the day so as not to have to do it later when you are more tired? Think it through.

And while preparing meals, why not make two instead of one? It take no longer, and if you can make two meatloaves, or two casseroles, or a double batch of soup and freeze one, why not do that and save having to make it twice? You will love yourself later!

And if you are cooking early in the day, why not set the table then, too? Why save that task until the last, busy minutes? How nice it is to walk into the kitchen to fix dinner and find the table is already set. Kim began letting her little boy, Alex, set the table while she fixed dinner to give him something to do. It wasn't long before he started doing that job all on his own without even being asked, he was so proud of his new job at only four years old.

Teach family members to always wash their hands before coming to the table. Most communicable diseases, such as flu and colds, are spread primarily by dirty hands. Just touching doorknobs, toys or computer keyboards can contaminate hands with thousands of invisible bacteria and viruses.

Make mealtime a very special time. Turn off the TV and turn on nice background music. Allow each child to take turns saying grace before the meal, teaching them not to be bashful to pray out loud. Use family mealtimes as opportunities to teach basic table manners, such as how to properly set the table and use their flatware, how to use a napkin, never chew with mouths open, and how to not leave the table until everyone is finished eating. What they do at the table on a daily basis is exactly what they will do when away. Teach them while they are young and good manners will be a matter of habit. Be sure to encourage everyone to talk about what they did today, their interests and their plans. Keep the conversation positive and free of criticism.

Treat your family like guests and they will actually look forward to dinner time with their family. Put fresh flowers on the table. Celebrate special occasions around the table, like holidays or an achievement like an excellent grade card. Take turns allowing each child to invite a friend to dinner. Invite other families over occasionally.

These are the little extras that make a wife and mother a teacher, and provides happy childhood memories. Not many homes today are fortunate enough to provide the nurturing environment that you can provide for your family by being an organized homemaker in the kitchen.

ACTION ASSIGNMENTS

- *Plan a Special Projects Day for reorganizing your kitchen.*
- *Decide which day of the week will be your day to plan menus, make a shopping list, and shop. Put it on your weekly calendar.*
- *See if you can complete a week's shopping without deviating from your written list. How much money did that save you?*
- *Plan for tomorrow night's dinner by thinking it through tonight.*
- *Surprise your family with a special dining room dinner, complete with tablecloth and fancy china, to celebrate some special occasion. Use it to honor someone in your family.*

— 13 —

TIME FOR YOU

Julie is a wonderful wife and mother, always there when her family needs her. She volunteers at school, is a Girl Scout leader, and teaches Sunday school. She is a top-notch homemaker and cook, too. But in spite of her reputation as a Superwoman, Julie feels that something is missing. Perhaps that is because Julie has never scheduled time for herself. Julie is running on empty.

Many, if not most, homemakers—whether they have an outside job or not—suffer from Julie's same problem. They do everything for everyone else, but not for themselves. Perhaps that's because they never put themselves on their own *"To Do List."* Maybe *"Take Care of Me"* should be right at the top of the list. Because every woman has needs on three levels:

1. Physical needs
2. Mental/Emotional needs
3. Spiritual Needs

Let's discuss ways to care for ourselves as much as we care for others in each of these areas.

LEVEL ONE: PHYSICAL NEEDS

Our bodies are very important. They are the only place we have to live until we die! Therefore we need to take good care of them so they don't die before we are ready. We need to maintain balance in that area of our lives, just like every other area, of course. It is out of balance to focus too much attention on our appetites, as much as it is to focus too little. It is just as bad to abuse our bodies with too much exercise as with not enough. It is foolish to spend an inordinate amount of time and/or money on dressing or improving our bodies cosmetically. In other words, we need to take our bodily needs seriously without allowing our bodily desires to rule over us.

We are to care for our bodies not primarily for our own interests, or to impress the world, but because it matters to God, who dwells inside our bodies.

"Or do you not know that your body is a temple of the Holy Spirit who is in you, whom you have from God, and that you are not your own? For you have been bought with a price: therefore glorify God in your body." (I Cor. 6:19,20)

When God dwelled in an earthly Temple, the people brought their tithes and offerings there-- heaping baskets of the first fruits of their harvests of crisp fresh fruits and vegetables, golden grains, and the healthiest kosher animals. All were offered as an act of worship to the Lord. Ever since the day of Pentecost, God has chosen instead to dwell inside of those who receive him as Lord of their lives in the form of the Holy Spirit. So every time you set food before yourself you are presenting an offering, of sorts, to God's temple—your own body.

WE ARE WHAT WE EAT

That means we must consider whether to foods we consume are worthy of a holy temple. Everything we eat needs to be not only acceptable to our taste buds, but an acceptable offering to the Lord—not because he is picky or demanding, but because he cares for us and our well-being. He also wants us to be fit and well enough to serve our family and others. We can be of no service to God when we are sickly. When we are not well we are forced to concentrate on taking care of ourselves until we recover. We can be of much greater service when we are healthy and energetic.

I am preaching to myself, here, being just as tempted to eat foolishly as the next woman. This may be the hardest area in which to discipline ourselves, but it is a goal we can accomplish if we take it one day, and one morsel, at a time. I have the habit of thinking to myself that what I am eating doesn't really count because *"tomorrow"* I will do better. I have finally accepted the fact that tomorrow never comes. It is what I eat *right now* that matters!

Try to eat only what will contribute to a healthy, energetic body. Concentrate on what is natural and farm-fresh as possible. One day I cooked a big pot of fresh string beans and onions flavored with ham only to be told, *"Wow—that was better than dessert!"* And it really was. Sip water with a slice of lemon or fresh juices rather than soda pop or *"juice"* drinks that are not 100% fruit juice. Eat two servings of fresh fruit per day. All of these things will contribute to your energy and improve your complexion. If you think fresh foods are too expensive, consider how costly it is to be sick!

BURNING CALORIES AT HOME

Another important step in caring for your physical needs is exercise. Yes, moving that body around is important, even though it just wants to sit. Our pastor once said, *"If you give your body its way, it will kill you!"* That is so true. The body is just made of flesh— and the flesh must be kept from taking over our lives. However, that does not mean we need to buy a membership to an exercise club or buy a lot of large, expensive exercise equipment.

Years ago when my mother-in-law moved to a new neighborhood, she said, *"Can you imagine what the lady next door does? She pays someone to clean her house. And then she pays to exercise at the health club! Now isn't that silly? She could clean her own house and get all the exercise she needs, and save the cost of the health club and the housekeeper!"*

Did you know that you can burn off just as many calories doing housework as you can by exercising on machines? You can expend as much energy behind a vacuum sweeper as you can behind a stationary bicycle. You can scrub the tub and shower instead of lifting weights. What offers more opportunities for exercise than your local gym? Your own home. Between sweeping, dusting, scrubbing, polishing, ironing, snow shoveling, , lawn mowing and weeding, there is hardly a muscle left unexercised.

For aerobic exercise try walking or biking in the neighborhood and exercise the dog at the same time. I like brisk walking because it is not damaging to the joints like jogging. It doesn't require any fancy equipment other than a decent pair of athletic shoes. In bad weather try walking indoors at the local shopping mall before hours—it is really busy there with fellow walkers!

Regular exercise benefits the body in many ways. It releases brain chemicals that help to eliminate emotional depression. Increased circulation strengthens the heart, helps your muscles assume their proper position and tone, helps your organs to function more smoothly, and even improves mental function and memory. I also find that exercise helps me get a much better night's sleep.

IT'S OKAY TO NAP

Speaking of sleep, I admit it. I just woke from an afternoon nap. Some days I just need a nap to get through what I call the second shift of the day. If I don't take that nap I drag around very slowly and unproductively. So why fight it?

I noticed that *"nap time"* is quite a tradition in certain European countries. They even close stores and banks for an hour or more in the middle of the day so everyone can eat lunch and take that much needed power nap. Why don't we do that in America? Well, that's one more advantage of having a homemaker-at-home career—you can sneak one in whenever you want!

I have read so many articles about how to get more accomplished by sleeping fewer hours. They even tell you how to set your clock earlier and earlier by little increments so you won't really miss that extra sleep time. But who do they think they are kidding? Your body knows when it is fatigued, and it will let you know, with less productivity, a less-than-optimal attitude (crabby anyone?) and lowered resistance to infections. Your body keeps score and eventually demands sleep repayment.

So why do that to yourself? I'd rather sleep more and yet be more energetic and productive when I am awake. If I hit a tired afternoon slump I have no qualms about grabbing a nap. I wake up refreshed and ready to go full speed again—and accomplish much more than if I had just pushed myself until bedtime.

In the delightful book <u>First We Have Coffee</u>, author Margaret Jensen tells how her mother raised a houseful of children with much faith, frugality and ingenuity. Yet as industrious as she was, every afternoon she napped. She needed it to bridge the busy hours from early morning to late evening. Small children notwithstanding, she took that nap!

A neurologist at the University of Ottawa stated, *"People are biologically wired for one nap a day, typically in mid-afternoon."* He also said, *"People whose jobs require a high level of vigilance...should be allowed to take scheduled naps. It may be the best way to improve their alertness, productivity, and overall performance."* Can you think of a job that requires more vigilance than that of a mother?

Research by the Sleep Disorders and Research Center of Detroit's Henry Ford Hospital confirms our need for rest. They proved with test subjects that increasing sleeping time by two hours a night (from seven up to nine hours of sleep per night) resulted in increased work performance scores. According to the research director, *"People appear to benefit from getting as much sleep as they can."* So be sure to schedule enough sleep time for yourself at night and maybe in the afternoon, too.

WHO'S IN CONTROL?

If you don't control your body, it will surely control you. Does your body tell the world that it is in control, or you are? The Bible tells us that it is our own choice whether we are controlled by the *"flesh"* or the *"Spirit."* It is our own choice, every minute of every day.

"Do not be deceived, God is not mocked; for whatever a man sows, this he will also reap. For the one who sows to his own flesh shall from the flesh reap corruption, but the one who sows to the Spirit shall from the Spirit reap eternal life." (Gal.6: 7,8)

I saw the truth of that scripture every day when I worked as an R.N. in the intensive care unit of a hospital. I cared for people who were reaping at the end of their lives what they had sown for many years. The smoker with emphysema or lung cancer, the alcoholics with cirrhosis of the liver, and the obese with failing organs throughout their bodies—all had bodies *"reaping corruption."*

Such loss of control over one's body doesn't happen overnight. It happens one day at a time until it becomes a controlling habit, or addiction. An old proverb says, *"Habits are first cobwebs, then cables."* Fortunately, old negative habits can be changed—also one day at a time—until they become new, positive habits.

If you have a negative habit that you want to change, you can. You can do all things through Christ who strengthens you! (Phil. 4:13) First, confess to God that you are sorry and need His help to change. Then make a moment-by-moment decision to live in the Spirit, rather than be controlled by your flesh.

"Walk by the Spirit, and you will not carry out the desire of the flesh. For the flesh sets its desire against the Spirit, and the Spirit against the flesh; for these are in opposition to one another, so that you may not do the things that you please... Now those who belong to Christ Jesus have crucified the flesh with its passions and desires. If we live by the Spirit, let us also walk by the Spirit." (Gal. 5: 16,17,24,25)

When we offer our bodies to God as a *"living sacrifice,"* He gives them back to us to enjoy—healthy and full of energy! That helps us to be happier and more successful at whatever we do. And that makes God happy, too.

LEVEL TWO: MENTAL/EMOTIONAL NEEDS

What would you do right now if you could do anything you wanted to? Would you go biking? Would you take a nap in the hammock in the back yard? Or eat a sack lunch in a pretty park, all by yourself? Or maybe you would just spend a few hours creating a quilt in your sewing room? Next question: When is the last time you actually did your favorite thing? Can you even remember?

I hate to be trite, but truly, *"All work and no play make Mommy a dull girl!"* Have you ever gotten so bogged down in day after week after month of just managing the home and taking care of children that you feel like you have become the mental equivalent of a two-year-old? Have you ever, like I once did, absentmindedly reached across your husband's plate at dinner and started cutting up his meat for him—right in front of his parents? *Awkward!* When you sink to that level, you begin to wonder if that brain of yours can still be salvaged. But, rejoice, it can!

However, it will take some effort on your part— effort to force yourself to make time for purely *"frivolous"* activities, just because you enjoy them. Take the time to do favorite non-productive things, like listening to old Christmas music while sorting through family photographs. Take yourself out on a date with yourself to the art museum. See if you can manage to spend an hour just counting the clouds from your patio recliner, or walking through the woods, or doodling on pretty papers. Do something you used to enjoy as a child when you hadn't a worry in the world or a deadline to meet.

We all need to take the time to enjoy the two things that every woman needs about as much as fish need water: *Beauty* and *Creativity*. When women don't have time to experience those things, it shrivels the soul. That is why so many women enjoy creating pretty gifts, or baking an artful cake, or placing a bunch of fresh flowers in a vase. We must feed that inner feminine need. So take time to be creative in whatever genre you desire, whether it is gardening, decorating, making crafts, sewing, painting, writing, or whatever. One of the fringe benefits of being a homemaker is that you can incorporate creativity and beauty into every aspect of your daily work, from sprucing up the house to preparing meals to clothing your family. Instead of approaching these activities as a *"duty"*, think of them as creative outlets!

Also take the time to learn something new. Sign up for a gourmet cooking class, take a college class on photography, or learn how to hand dye and spin yarn. We must do something to knock the cobwebs out of our heads, to meet new people, and to just spend time alone with ourselves as well. Over my lifetime I have never passed up an opportunity to learn something new and different, whether a new skill or a new way of looking at the world. I have learned such crafty things as how to knit, crochet, quilt, embroider, needle-felt and sew. I have learned Chinese cooking, various forms of artwork, gardening, jewelry making and public speaking. I even learned how to fly a hot-air balloon. Right there in your own hometown there are many things you can learn, whether at the local community college, at the library, or by joining a club.

Regarding indulging in beauty—how about your own? Schedule a regular weekly *"Tune-Up Time"* for yourself. Make it your special time to primp and preen. Perhaps every Thursday night you can have your husband put the children to bed while you take a long soak in a hot bubble bath. Make it a luxurious event, complete with dim lights, a scented candle and quiet music. Soak until your fingertips are all wrinkly. After your bath slather on perfumed lotion, then condition and brush your hair, and give yourself a manicure and pedicure. You will feel beautiful all week long, and your husband will enjoy the new you, too.

Above all, take time to laugh. Check out an old movie like <u>The Gods Must Be Crazy</u> and watch it until you have tears of laughter running down your face. Play the game our sons used to enjoy most, *"Stinky Socks,"*

164

where you play tag by chasing each other with someone's smelly, dirty sock. It was hilarious. Or spend time with a friend who always gives you the giggles. Watch re-runs of <u>America's Funniest Videos</u> until your sides ache. It is important to laugh because it is very good for your health and your psyche. *"A merry heart doeth good like a medicine."* (Prov. 17:22)

Postponing fun until tomorrow is a mistake, because today is the only day you ever have to enjoy it. Tomorrow you may need it for whatever lies ahead. My favorite season is autumn. I love the excitement of crisp, cool days and brilliant hillsides and crunching leaves underfoot. Taking a long drive through the countryside or a brisk walk in the park fills me with anticipation and exuberance. But I've often let an entire fall season slip by without taking a single afternoon to enjoy it, just because I was *"busy"* and thought I could do it *"tomorrow."* Before I knew it, it was winter, and I had missed what could never be retrieved.

What is your favorite season? What is your favorite pastime? What would you most love to do right this moment, even if just for a few minutes? Why don't you go ahead and just do it, right now?   And make it a regular part of your life.

LEVEL THREE: SPIRITUAL NEEDS

How many people do you know of who have it all together, have everything they want and need, and yet are still unhappy and unsatisfied? From the rich and famous to the person next door, or even inside our own skin, this can be the sad reality. No amount of organization, or talent, or money can make us happy if we neglect this last—but most important—need.

We need a real relationship with the real God. That same One who created us, gave us life and breath, and watches us daily, will not come into our life uninvited. With Him people can be happy with very little else. Without Him, all the blessings in the world fail to satisfy. It would be a shame to search for happiness in every other way than where the true source of peace and joy originates, in our Creator.

Lisa was a case in point. She had everything we all wish we had—a loving husband and children, a huge home in a wealthy neighborhood, a BMW convertible, big diamonds, and great health. She was good looking, had everything and could do anything she wanted. Yet Lisa was miserable. She told me that she often suffered from depression. And even when she wasn't depressed she was unsatisfied. Nothing pleased her. When she came home from a lovely vacation I asked her if she had a good time. *"No,"* she whined. *"I couldn't find anything to buy."*

Lisa was a classic example of someone who searched in all the wrong places for something to fill that empty *"God shaped vacuum"* with everything *except* God. No matter how I tried to convince her that she needed to fill her inner emptiness with Him, she would not listen. Lisa chose to leave Self on the throne of her life than to turn her life over to the Lord of Life, Jesus Christ, and put Him there instead. She preferred being the one in charge, even though that wasn't working very well for her. The last I knew, Lisa was carrying on an adulterous affair and wasn't any happier.

But most women who don't know Jesus as Lord are not like Lisa. They are usually not spoiled or self-centered. They are usually decent, well-meaning people who are doing the best they can to live a good life. They just don't realize that living a good life is not enough to make them happy, now or ever, for more than a few fleeting moments. They are up and down, like a roller coaster, happy one minute, unhappy the next. They are completely unaware, or unconcerned, that Jesus said, *"I am the Way, and the Truth, and the Life. No one comes to the Father except through Me."* (John 14:6)

Perhaps you are one of those women who has never paused to consider those words. *What if they are true?* Why is it that every time you write today's date, you are actually testifying to how many years it has been since Jesus died on the cross for your salvation? Could that just be a coincidence, or is it God's design as a divine reminder of Who loves you most of all?

Why does everyone, and every religion, agree that Jesus was a good man and a prophet if, indeed, He was lying about Who He really is? He claimed to be the Messiah, the human incarnation of Father God on earth, the only one who can forgive our sins, and the only door to eternal life in heaven! Who on earth can afford to ignore such claims?

There is one way to find out if Jesus is who He claims to be. You can ask Him to show you. Just say, *"Lord Jesus, I don't know if You are really who You claim to be, but if You are, please show me. If you can really wash away my sins through Your shed blood on the cross, please wash away mine. I know I have hurt myself and others in my life. I know I have violated Your commandments. I know I am guilty of sins I cannot take back. I will give you my life, as You have given Your life for mine. If You can really come into my heart, please fill me with Your Holy Spirit. Lead me into all Truth. Help me to truly know You, follow You, and live a humble and repentant life before You."*

If you pray that prayer right now, your life will never be the same. I know. Because I did it one day, decades ago, and everything changed. I was surprised by Love such as I had never experienced it. I was a teenager then, and today I am old. But that was the single most important moment of my life. It will be yours also. Go with God, and be very blessed as a homemaker, a wife and mother, and as a woman of faith. You will experience a much richer, more meaningful life, and will look forward to heavenly eternity with your Creator on that day when He takes you home for good.

Made in the USA
Coppell, TX
06 February 2024

28665241R00098